THERE IS somethir
in the air. Bookshop
setting up whole se
covering subjects li
change the world fo
reduce our carbon
live an ethical lifesty
shop in a socially re
way. National news
have green and eth
columns. For birthd
of us are buying go
water pumps for ou
and relatives than e

It is ordinary pe
doing everyday thin
like shopping, eatin
reading who are ma
difference. Superm
launch fair trade ranges
because that's what more
and more consumers want
to buy. Energy companies
invest in renewables because
consumers demand greener
electricity. Companies
recycle more, plant trees to
offset their carbon output
and publish ethical policies
because without these
measures, more and more of

faster those chances will
come about.

This guide is for anyone
who wants to spend the
70,000 hours of their potential
working life doing something
that makes the world a better
place, or at least doesn't
contribute to its destruction.
We haven't attempted to

overnight, but change is
definitively in the air. Why not
use your working life to make
it happen?

Gideon Burrows
Editor

For more features, special reports
and news on ethical careers
visit **ethicalcareers.org**, where
you can also register for our free
monthly email newsletter.

FOREWORD

natracare®

healthier by nature

She knows why...

more women, just like her, are choosing Natracare organic cotton tampons and totally chlorine-free natural pads and liners.

because today's women seek to restrict their contact with synthetics, plastic, unnecessary chemicals and additives - their natural first choice in feminine hygiene is the gynaecologist recommended, Natracare products.

Natracare tampons are made of only certified organic, 100% pure cotton and our full range of sanitary pads and panty liners are made from only totally chlorine-free, natural and biodegradable materials.

Available at Boots, Waitrose, Sainsbury's, and all natural health shops.

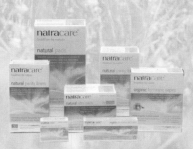

GETTING STARTED

WHY CHOOSE AN ETHICAL CAREER?

An introduction by **JOE SAXTON**, chair of campaign group People & Planet and chair of the Institute of Fundraising.

OVER THE last 20 years we have seen an explosion of ways in which ordinary people can make a difference to the world – organic food, fair trade products, green energy suppliers and ethical investments, to name a few. Now that interest has spread from how people spend their money to how they spend their time – particularly as employees.

Anybody thinking about an ethical career is making a clear statement about the kind of world they want to live in. And making sure that the values and fruits of our working life make the world a better place, rather than a worse one, is one of the most powerful statements that any individual can make.

This guide will help anybody who wants to decide how to spend their working life in an ethical way. But the story doesn't end there. Whole new specialist ethical career fields, even 'industries', are opening up. One is fundraising – practically unheard of 20 years ago.

The Institute of Fundraising represents over 4,000 individuals for whom fundraising for charities and campaign groups is central to their working life. It is among the most sophisticated and diverse types of career in the not-for-profit sector. The flexibility, the pay, and the range of causes that fundraisers raise money for make it a fantastic way to spend a working life. But fundraising is also an increasingly competitive environment in which to work. Every job opportunity is hard fought!

For many people, the precursor to an ethical career is a passion for justice and sustainability in the world around them. People & Planet is the UK's largest student-led organisation dedicated to the elimination of poverty and to the protection of human rights and the environment.

With nearly 150 groups at universities, sixth-form colleges and schools around the country and a regular action email that goes to more than 10,000 young people, we help people make a real difference through our campaigns. For those who want to find an ethical career, experience with People & Planet can provide the proof of a track record at interview.

Enjoy this guide. I hope you will find a career that matches your skills, expertise and passion. Together, we are all working to leave this world a better place. ❯

→**People and Planet**
www.peopleandplanet.org

→**Institute of Fundraising**
www.institute-of-fundraising.org.uk

What's your ideal ethical career?

Find out with our fun quiz.
Question master: **ADRIAN SANDIFORD**.

You're at a job interview when you're asked to outline your skills and interests. You tell the panel of three smiling people sitting in front of you that:

a You love to communicate with people, and enjoy the challenge of trying to change the way people think about things.

b Although you avidly follow ethical issues, you often find yourself attracted and intrigued by how the business world works.

c You think individuals matter more than policy. Changing the world should be about giving hands-on help to the people who need it.

You're reading a newspaper on the bus. Are you most likely to:

a Read out interesting facts to the person sitting next to you. The story you've just seen is too important to keep to yourself – this stranger needs to know what's going on!

b Turn straight to the business pages before moving on to read the social care section.

c Pass your paper to a forlorn-looking passenger with nothing to read, despite the fact you haven't finished with it yet. They clearly need it more than you do.

Think back to your time at school. While your hormones raged and exams came thick and fast, you still found the time to:

a Organise your entire year group in protest against the headmaster's attempt to reduce lunch break by ten minutes.

b Set up a student-run shop selling drinks and snacks, raising funds to redecorate the decrepit common room.

c Venture into town to help out at the understaffed community centre.

Your hero or heroine is:

a Legendary South African statesman, Nelson Mandela.

b Body Shop founder, Anita Roddick.

c The Crimean War's Lady of the Lamp, Florence Nightingale.

It's party time. It's your friend's birthday and you all head out for a meal before hitting the town. Inevitably, you're the one who ends up:

a Telling the waiters what a great person your friend is and singing everyone's praises with gusto.

b Picking up the end of meal cheque and gently sorting out who needs to pay what as the clear-cut rules of maths collapse into an incomprehensible mess.

c Making sure your friend who's had a few drinks too many – there's always one – is feeling up to going on or seeing whether you should help them home.

Your best friend wants to set you up on a date. You tell them that you're looking for someone who:

a Likes to talk and express themselves, is willing to consider new ideas, and has a good sense of humour.

b Appreciates the value of money, is graced with a warm heart, and has a good sense of humour.

c You can look after, is tender like the night, and has a good sense of humour.

So, how
did you do?

Ideally, you'd like your job to:

a Empower people to get their voices heard.

b Combine your passion for a cause with profit principles and business.

c Help people feel better or achieve, but on a one-to-one level.

If you scored mostly:

a You could consider a career in campaigning. You're concerned about issues, want to help people be heard, and are good at communicating a message. Why not volunteer with an organisation that works on a cause close to your heart, get involved, and see what you can offer. It could be the start of something beautiful.

b Why not consider a career in ethical business? You've got financial savvy coupled with a socially responsible outlook. It's a great combination with which to launch your own organisation marrying profit with progress. Alternatively, you could look into applying business models to existing charities or working within a corporate's CSR unit. Find out what works for you.

c How about a career on the front line: charity carer, social worker, or youth development? You've got a caring attitude, want to help people directly, and have the passion to make a difference to individual lives. Try giving your time to a local charity as the first step on the charity ladder.

AGAINST THE ODDS

Ethical careers are for everyone. So what if your CV isn't bulging with qualifications and charity experience? Start from the bottom and work upwards, writes **ADRIAN SANDIFORD**.

MANY OF today's most inspirational movers and shakers in socially responsible organisations worked their way up from humble beginnings. Like them, you don't need a Masters in Charity Management, or have trained for five years, to find your place in a long-lasting, rewarding ethical career.

"The clincher in starting out in charity work is to show personal commitment and empathy," says Paul Canal, managing director of recruitment agency Charity People.

Volunteering and temporary work are an excellent way to demonstrate your ability, dedication and desire to get involved. You can also acquire new skills, learn about the sector and pursue opportunities within your chosen organisation.

"You need to have the determination to put up with things and get your chance," says Canal. "But once you're inside a charity, you have the chance of moving within it – from the postroom to fundraising – or whatever area it is that you find interesting."

This isn't just recruitment rhetoric. If you're enthusiastic and patient enough to keep trying – and prove yourself to the right people – full-time work can be forthcoming. You could rise from sorting books in a charity shop to organising prestigious global events, such as the Tokyo leg of Live8 – just like Claire Lewis:

"I was volunteering because I wanted to do something different," says Claire, who is now Oxfam's international artiste liaison manager. Besides Live8, she

worked on Make Poverty History's 'click' adverts, featuring the likes of Brad Pitt, Cameron Diaz, Liam Neeson and Kanye West. "It's been amazing – the pinnacle of my career."

Claire was 21 when she started volunteering in her local Oxfam shop. Within a year, she had risen to shop manager and began working in a number of Oxfam branches across London. Volunteering became employment. On the second time of applying, Claire was offered a job as fundraising assistant. "It was hard, a really difficult time," she says. "But the shop volunteering definitely helped me get a foot in the door."

The fundraising job involved a lot of admin – not her dream career – but Claire used the opportunity to learn more about the charity, take on greater responsibility and shift up a gear in terms of management. "It gave me a really good grounding and the confidence to go forward," she says. "Oxfam is really willing to train from within, and if you're bright, helpful, and useful, there's lots of opportunity. A huge number of volunteers move up through the organisation."

With experience and on-the-job learning behind her, Claire got a position as major donors officer at Friends of the Earth, later moving to a similar post at Plan International before returning to Oxfam – significantly higher up the career ladder than when she started. Having been there and done it, what advice does she have for the next generation?

"Get involved as a volunteer," she says. "Try and see what's available so, as a volunteer, you can position yourself in the right place and develop your skills in that area. You can't just arrive at these jobs – you have to demonstrate your commitment and understanding of the organisation. Be prepared to do work that is tedious and boring. I spent a year shifting through loads of second-hand clothes. Now my job's extremely demanding, but also exhilarating."

Canal agrees that volunteering is a good starting point. "It demonstrates you care and are actively engaged," he says, adding that the financial burden of working for free

can be eased by balancing volunteering with a part-time paid job, like bar work.

An alternative is to land that dream job via temporary work. What may start out as short-term, somewhat uninspiring work can – with perseverance, ambition, and ability – lead to much greater things.

Diana Gayle joined the Fairtrade Foundation as a general admin temp. But she knuckled down and impressed her employers into giving her a permanent job. After four promotions in four years, the 28-year-old is now the organisation's non-food manager. Recent responsibilities include managing the UK launch of Fairtrade certified cotton. That's some serious career progression.

"I pushed every boundary I could, at every possible opportunity," says Diana. "I was very keen to start at the bottom and learn as much as possible, to absorb things like a sponge. I was encouraged by my employers and increasingly took on more responsibility."

Diana's key advice following her own experience is to be proactive: "Your

employers will recognise if you put yourself in a position to learn and are committed to doing things. Make sure you let people know you're looking to take on more responsibility. Let them see how you work and show yourself to be an asset. Be enthusiastic, energetic, and give everything you've got."

Charities are not the only destination for ethically minded jobseekers. There are plenty of ways of making a difference – even in the private sector.

Gary Bruce had no idea he'd find himself in what he regards as ethical employment when he joined Sainsbury's as a schoolleaver. His first job was as a Saturday shop assistant. Today, he's the company's charitable affairs manager, having worked his way up the ranks and across divisions.

CSR from a major supermarket is a matter of opinion. But since joining Sainsbury's CSR team, Gary believes he's been involved with numerous worthy projects, including the expansion of the company's food-donation scheme – where surplus stock is donated to homeless charities.

Despite the chasm between Sainsbury's and the Fairtrade Foundation, Gary's advice echoes that of Diana: "The opportunities are there if you want them – just don't expect someone to manage your career for you," he says.

"When I felt I was unsatisfied with my role, I looked for something else. I stepped over the divide from retail and am working with less fortunate people. So you've got to have a passion for something, but it's only going to happen if you want it to."

It's not always easy to change the world. But with the right attitude, commitment, and a desire to seize opportunities, you could soon be making a real difference. What are you waiting for? ◗

→ **Sainsbury's CSR department**
www.j-sainsbury.co.uk/csr

→ **The Fairtrade Foundation**
www.fairtrade.org.uk

→ **Charity People**
www.charitypeople.co.uk

→ **Oxfam**
www.oxfam.org.uk

WORKING
WITH
PEOPLE

CHARITY BEGINS AT HOME

You don't have to go abroad to change the world. A career in the UK charity sector could be more rewarding than you think, says **PAUL CANAL**, chief executive of Charity People.

ETHICAL CAREERS have never been more popular. Wall Street's culture of greed has been usurped by Drop the Debt. The Make Poverty History campaign and Live8 have created an avalanche of interest in careers in the charity or not-for-profit sectors.

But the challenge is to convert this current passion into something sustainable. A movement for a brighter world that will continue after Geldof, wrist bands and Coldplay have left the stage.

One thing is certain. This shouldn't mean tens of thousands of keen young things flying around in ozone-gobbling jets to smile warmly at the world's poor. Our own desire to work in international development often sits uncomfortably with the need for the developing world to engage in capacity building on its own terms.

Some excellent schemes do provide opportunities to engage with the developing world with integrity. But there are also boundless opportunities to create change by working here in Britain, in our own not-for-profit sector, working and campaigning on both a national and international basis.

Medécins sans Frontières, well known for its medical work in war zones, following disasters and in some of the poorest communities in the world, recently announced it was opening UK centres, so serious has the problem of health exclusion here become. Literacy rates in many of our poor schools compare unfavourably to most of Europe, and are much worse than Cuba.

Against this backdrop, we have a thriving national not-for-profit sector, with thousands of local and national organisations engaging directly with those in need here and abroad. There are almost unlimited volunteering opportunities, as well as a wealth of paid opportunities – and well-paid ones too! The opportunity for personal development and advancement in the voluntary sector often exceeds that offered by many private sector organisations.

So, how do you go about getting your career in the voluntary sector? A background of involvement in charities or volunteering will give you a head start. A willingness to do voluntary or temporary work will strengthen your CV while increasing your experience and knowledge base. Flexibility in the type of work, organisation or location you're willing to work in will enhance your chances of success.

Jobs websites, including our own, and sector jobs and volunteering events like Forum3 are a good way to discover what's out there. Most importantly, use your own networks – college, friends and family – to search out opportunities.

Career prospects are good, pay is improving and opportunities are expanding, but the real reward is the knowledge that your career could play a part in making the world a better place for all its current and future inhabitants. ▶

Working for a Better World is a comprehensive guide to working in the UK charity and voluntary sector. Published by the UK Voluntary Sector Workforce Hub, it is available for £5.

→**UK Voluntary Sector**
www.ukworkforcehub.org.uk

→**CharityPeople**
www.charitypeople.com

→**Forum3, the not-for-profit recruitment event**
www.forum3.co.uk

HELPLINE CASE WORKER

Name: Georgina Bream
Age: 21

So, what exactly do you do?

I work for the National Missing Persons Helpline. It provides support for families of missing people. We never give up on a case and people feel they can turn to us when they don't know what to do about a missing relative. Even if we can't help in a particular situation, we can always provide advice as to what to do next.

How did you get into this job?

I saw it advertised in The Big Issue. Although I did not have specific helpline experience, I had experience in the voluntary sector – I had worked in the care industry during school and university holidays, and volunteered for a local homeless charity after I finished my degree. I also carefully researched the charity so that I had a full understanding of their services, history and mission statement.

What does your typical day involve?

Every case that the charity registers is assigned a case manager. My role is to support their work. This means, day-to-day, I'm implementing searches for missing people and speaking to all those involved – be it police, family or social services.

What's the most memorable experience you've had in this job?

The first time I answered the phone to a missing person who we had found was very memorable. It had taken the person a long time to pluck up the courage to ring in.

Best things about the job?

Knowing that you are providing support to families of missing people in a tough time, and that you are actively contributing to solving their problem. The atmosphere in the office is also really nice – you can tell that everyone works here because they enjoy what they do. We resolve 70 percent of the cases we work on, so job satisfaction is really tangible.

Any top tips for someone wanting to get into this work?

Volunteering for a helpline is probably the best way to see whether this is something that you want to do. Some people find taking calls upsetting, so it's good to know your limits in an unpaid capacity first. Volunteering in general – even if it is just for one afternoon a week – is probably the best way to gain experience. ▶

National Missing Persons Helpline
t. 020 8392 4518
e. info@missingpersons.org
www.missingpersons.org

CHILDREN'S CENTRE MANAGER

Name: Melanie Mayers
Age: 20

So, what do you actually do? I'm in charge of the day-to-day running of an after-school club for children aged 4-11. My job is to ensure everything runs smoothly and to deal with any problems that might arise, whether it's a behavioural issue or a parent arriving late to pick up their child.

What makes your job so ethical? Kids' City is a charity that fundraises in order to keep costs down for parents. Every child's place at the after-school clubs and holiday schemes is subsidised. Further subsidies are available for parents on a low income.

Did you do any specific training or qualifications to get this job? Most of the courses I did at college are relevant to this job in one way or another. I did Sports Science and Drama A-levels, a community sports leader award, a youth work course and first aid training. Since joining Kids' City I've completed a course on working with children with disabilities, health and safety, food hygiene and an NVQ Level 3 in Playwork.

What does your typical day involve? I arrive at the school at about 3pm along with the other playworkers and volunteers. We get the room and equipment ready for the children. They have a snack before dividing up for their chosen activities, which might be anything from tae kwon do to cookery, homework to hairdressing, or just playing games outside. They then have a chance to play until their parents pick them up. I'm always kept busy!

What's the most memorable experience you've had in this job? During the summer playschemes, we run 'Breakout' trips where we take the children to the countryside or museums. Seeing their faces when they first saw the dinosaurs at the Natural History Museum was amazing.

And the most challenging? Knowing how to deal with children with behavioural difficulties. You don't always want to be the bad guy, but at the same time, the children need to learn to behave for the safety of others.

What are your plans for the future? I'll probably stay at Kids' City for a while longer and then go to teacher training college. I love working with kids. ◗

→**Kids' City**
t. 020 8683 9600
e. info@kidscity.org.uk
www.kidscity.org.uk

BUILDING A BETTER FUTURE

With property prices on the rise, and demand outstripping supply, there are more and more opportunities to work in organisations that provide affordable housing solutions. **ROSE SMITH** reports.

HAVE YOU ever stopped to think about the roof over your head? Imagine if you wanted to buy that property, on your own, and on a current low, or even non-existent salary. Chances are you wouldn't be able to afford it, unless you had help from a parent or received an unexpected windfall. You wouldn't be alone. Many people don't own their own home because of low incomes, poor credit ratings that block a mortgage application or, most crucially, because of the housing shortage affecting this country.

The crisis of demand outstripping supply (with an estimated 210,000 new properties needed every year, and only 154,000 built in the past five) means that rising prices are squeezing public-sector workers out of urban areas where they are needed most. Lower-income families are being forced onto longer waiting lists for local authority accommodation.

Fortunately, the government has recognised the problem, and is calling on the housing sector to come up with solutions. Under the Pathfinders scheme, nine areas of the UK will receive huge sums of investment to create new homes. Of these, a proportion will be so-called 'affordable housing', managed by a diverse

and energetic body of organisations in the not-for-profit and charitable sectors.

The housing sector has responded to the government's demand for decent housing – defined as "warm, weatherproof and with reasonably modern facilities" in several ways. And it employs 80,000 people in a diverse range of jobs to meet the objectives, from urban designers, coming up with affordable housing that doesn't compromise on style, to policy and research officers identifying trends in housing and social policy, or operations managers overseeing eco-housing projects.

Social housing, which accounts for 20 percent of

Photo: © Hockerton Housing Project

English households, provides long-term rental for low-income families and those with special needs. This type of housing used to be provided by local authorities, but since the 1980s, not-for-profit organisations called 'housing associations' have taken over the management and construction of council-housing stock.

There are more than 1,500 housing associations in England, managing around two million homes, and with assets valued at £51bn in 2001. The most common job role within an association is housing officer, where duties include supporting residents'

groups and identifying necessary maintenance work.

Housing associations are also the main providers of new affordable homes through key-worker schemes, which allow public-sector workers, such as nurses and teachers, to take loans towards the cost of a property, or shared-ownership schemes, where you buy a share of the property and pay rent on the remaining share that you don't own.

Roles here could vary from administering applications to liaising with the Housing Corporation, which oversees and funds associations in England.

This public-sector body is one of the largest employers in the sector, with around 500 staff based in nine offices. Benefits are good, with training, sponsorship towards professional qualifications, career breaks and even bicycle loans as part of the package.

Although housing associations are major suppliers of affordable housing, charities, environmental groups and design companies also play a role in this diverse field. Wayne Hemingway, co-founder of clothing store Red or Dead, now runs Hemingwaydesign,

a company specialising in affordable and social design and currently working on a large housing scheme in north London. He believes there is a misconception that housing isn't a glamorous career.

"We need to get the message across that people who are interested in housing really can give something back. A designer's job on this earth is to make things better for the majority not just a privileged minority."

Environmental groups that construct and develop eco-housing are another player in the field, offering opportunities for a challenging career.

One such company is the Hockerton Housing Project, a self-sufficient ecological housing development in Nottinghamshire. The residents' houses generate their own clean energy, harvest their own water and recycle waste materials causing no pollution or carbon dioxide emissions.

There are nine people involved in the project, all of whom are graduates, including marketing and media manager, Nick White. He spent ten years in the pharmaceutical industry before moving across to an ethical career. With a further ten years away from the

private sector under his belt, he reflects that a career in sustainable housing is "less about money and more about work that is meaningful".

A move between sectors cost him a 75 percent drop in salary but he found that his change of lifestyle meant he needed less money to live. "I don't have to treat myself to expensive holidays and house extensions because I'm so stressed at work, like many of my friends and former colleagues," he says.

Another example of an environmental housing organisation is BioRegional Development Group. Best known for building the UK's largest eco-village, Bed-Zed, in Wallington, Surrey, the group provides a mix of social housing, shared ownership, key-worker homes and private houses. Demonstrating how the housing sector is working hand-in-glove with government, the group has a new project in partnership with conservation charity WWF to create homes for 5,000 people in the Thames Gateway regeneration area as part of the Pathfinders scheme. BioRegional employs 25 staff and jobs vary from scientific, such as waste researcher, to core support, such as communications manager.

If this sounds like your dream employer, you might be cheered to know that an environmental background isn't necessarily a pre-requisite to get a job there, says Sumwet Manchanda, director of BioRegional Consulting. "When we recruit, we do look for candidates with an environmental management qualification, but we also consider those from related sectors such as planning, architecture or business management, who can have an environmental bent of mind and a passion for the subject," he says.

One way of demonstrating this passion is through work experience. As Nick White says, "Graduates should gain some practical experience rather than coming straight off the theoretical university production line." For the environmental housing sector, this could be through volunteering for organisations such as Willing Workers on Organic Farms or BTCV.

Further study can also quicken your career progression, according to Bright Futures, Bright Lives, Bright Careers, a free CD-ROM that contains an abundance of information for anyone looking to begin a career in housing. The Chartered Institute of Housing runs a Graduate Conversion Course, either as distance learning or part time, and often partially paid for by employers. At the end of the course, trainees get an accreditation from the institute, which opens the door to specialising in one field.

If you are changing careers, Bright Futures recommends emphasising the following skills: good customer handling, team working, liaison with outside agencies, and the ability to work to deadlines and to supervise, manage and co-ordinate workers. The Housing Corporation says it looks for employees who understand that housing is about more than just putting a roof over people's heads. It is a sector that provides diversity and a career that offers the chance to make a difference: to individuals, communities and the environment. ▶

→**Bioregional Development Group**
www.bioregional.com

→**Bright Futures, Bright Lives, Bright Careers**
www.brightfutures.uk

→**Chartered Institute of Housing**
www.cih.org

→**Hockerton Housing Project**
www.hockerton.demon.co.uk

→**Housing Corporation**
www.housingcorp.gov.uk

HOMELESS PROJECT MANAGER

Name: David Hewitt
Age: 28

What makes your job so ethical? I'm a project manager at Crisis, one of the UK's largest homelessness organisations. People who have experienced homelessness are some of the most excluded in our society and there are often complex issues that have contributed to their situation. We provide positive services that remove obstacles and help them to build the confidence and skills needed to take control of their own lives.

How did you get into this job? After gaining office experience from temping in the private sector, I got a foot in the door at Crisis in an entry-level admin position. Since then, I have gained experience working on a range of projects, often through putting myself forward for extra responsibility and volunteering opportunities. I think this was down to genuine interest in the work rather than part of any career 'master plan'. I've also been fortunate to work for an organisation that is willing to take a chance on helping people progress.

What does your typical day involve? I spend a lot of time travelling around the UK visiting homelessness organisations, meeting with local council representatives, frontline staff and clients. I select partners for new projects that we are planning and provide them with funding, training and support to ensure that they are delivering services that meet our clients' needs.

What kind of personality is best suited to working in a job like yours? You need to be a bit of a diplomat, able to communicate with a diverse mix of people, and it's essential that you're non-judgemental. People often aren't what they seem. More importantly, you don't know what they're capable of achieving if given the opportunity.

Any top tips for someone wanting to get into this work? Volunteering is a great way to gain experience and there are plenty of opportunities to volunteer. Once you're in the right area, if you've got enthusiasm and a willingness to muck in, you can progress – your first job needn't be your dream job. ▶

→**Crisis**
t. 0870 11 33 35
e. enquiries@crisis.org.uk
www.crisis.org.uk

YOUTH WORKER

Name: Dawn Oliver
Age: 35

So, what do you actually do? I work with young people at a Fairbridge project in Solent, Southampton. These young people are not accessing any form of education, training or employment and we provide them with the support and confidence to believe in themselves, their abilities and their skills to change their own lives for the better.

What makes your job so ethical? Young people come to us from a range of backgrounds and experiences. Very often they arrive with low self-esteem and a lack of confidence.

My job is to show them that, regardless of where they are in their lives, they have something of value to the rest of the world.

How did you get into this job? I left school aged 16 and started working straight away. In my mid-twenties I went to college to do a diploma in Outdoor Activities. Since then I have returned to college and got a Diploma in Client-Centred Counselling. I worked for not-for-profit organisations in the USA, helping young people from New York. When I returned to the UK, I worked in youth clubs, information and advice centres, an emotional and behavioural difficulties school and as a residential social worker. I then went back to college and started working for Fairbridge.

What does your typical day involve? There is never a typical day working with these young people, their lives are so hectic. I'll spend time talking with agencies to find out what's out there for young people. I'll take part in sessions to build relationships, which are key to this job. I spend a lot of time with young people,

one-to-one, talking about their plans and dreams, setting aims and going to appointments with them.

What's the most memorable experience you've had in this job? The achievements of young people are always memorable. It's the little things: the first time they look you in the eye, or use someone's name, offer to share something or make tea, assert themselves or engage in banter.

Best things about the job? The young people. Seeing them change, become more confident as they achieve things, and start to think positively about themselves and others.

And the most challenging? The nature of young people's lives can make it quite hard to plan far in advance. The negative image that they receive means they're not as readily accepted as they could be. ❯

→**Fairbridge**
t. 020 7928 1704
e. info@fairbridge.org.uk
www.fairbridge.org.uk

EVENTS AND FORUMS MANAGER

Name: Kate Paisley
Age: 24

So, what do you actually do? I work in Harrogate & Area Council for Voluntary Service (CVS), which aims to support and promote the local voluntary and community sector. Within the CVS I run eight forums that bring together individuals, service users, representatives from voluntary groups, and local government bodies to discuss issues relating to various topics, such as mental health or domestic abuse. The forums ensure that, with input from people who work in that area or use the services, things are planned appropriately.

I also organise any events that may come up through the forums, such as events for cancer patients, their relatives and carers about local cancer services. This involves everything from booking the venue and planning the programme to organising speakers and publicity.

What kind of personality is best suited to a job like yours? Someone who is creative, enjoys a challenge and who thrives on working in a very flexible and varied environment. You need to be good at organising your time as you can be working on a variety of things at the same time, so might need to 'swap hats' several times a day.

What skills and experience do you need to work in this sector? Communication skills are very important. A lot of my work revolves around going to meetings and expressing ideas or opinions. So, you need to be confident in communicating with people at different levels. Organisation and a proactive approach are important, as well as good IT skills.

What are your plans for the future? This job has introduced me to a range of areas of work, many of which appeal for the future. I enjoy planning events and helping people to influence service planning. I also really enjoy development work and the publicity aspect of my role.

Any top tips for someone wanting to get into this work? Get into the sector in whatever way you can, be it by volunteering or an administrative post. Gain some experience and make contacts. If you can, volunteer in an area you would like to work in — you will gain invaluable knowledge and experience that will be useful when positions come up. ◗

→**Harrogate & Area Council for Voluntary Service**
t. 01423 504 074
e. cvs@harrogate.org
www.harrogate.org

LAUGHTER, ALONG WITH TEARS

Consider a career with substance misuse charity, **ADDACTION**.

> For me, one of Addaction's finest assets is that each member is a piece of the puzzle.

ADDACTION IS the UK's leading charity working solely in the field of drug and alcohol treatment. Founded in 1967, it now has over 70 services employing some 700 staff from Glasgow to Penzance, and across the UK. Clients at Addaction come from all backgrounds and ages, some with long-term addiction and dependency problems. Their needs are assessed and a programme is provided, to help them work their way towards abstinence or harm reduction.

Staff come from all backgrounds and ages too – indeed, a common misconception is that a member of the team needs a background in tackling substance misuse. In fact,

> I love the work. It includes laughter along with the tears.

transferable skills are the real key to our success. It all adds to Addaction's growing expertise. That's what helps make real differences to the lives of people with substance misuse problems.

"In my experience," says Guy Pink, Addaction's HR director, "what makes Addaction different is the way in which a fully externally accredited training programme is provided to all frontline staff and to all managers, covering everything from drug awareness to counselling techniques to IT skills. This training gives people the intensive, hands-on

knowlecge they need to work with our clients.

"There's often an assumption that, as we're a charity, staff will not receive any benefits over and above pay and pensions," says Guy. "But as well as paying a competitive salary, we offer many other rewards and benefits to our staff. Performance-related pay and management bonuses line up next to a generous annual leave allowance: a minimum of 28 days for all staff, plus the usual statutory holidays.

"Staff also benefit in other ways: a support service is provided both to staff and their families through an Employee Assistance Programme," adds Guy. "This programme offers support with everything from home relationships to work issues, and is, of course, completely confidential. We are also really committed to equality and diversity and have a number of flexible working arrangements in place".

In all respects, Addaction remains at the cutting edge of good practice and innovation in the field of alcohol and drug misuse treatment. We aspire to be at the cutting edge when it comes to our staff, too. We'll provide you with the support, training and opportunity you need to further your career with us. ▶

addaction

Helping individuals and communities to manage the effects of drug and alcohol misuse

Project administrator

You'll provide a wide range of support to the managers and team of our specialist drug and alcohol projects. You'll be skilled in word processing, correspondence, email, database maintenance, co-ordinating diaries and liaising with staff, volunteers and external bodies.

In other words, you'll ensure the smooth running of the office and maintain a safe, friendly environment both for staff and clients.

Project worker

You'll provide support, information and advice to individuals in relation to substance misuse in a structured and safe setting.

But not only that – you'll also improve access to appropriate services for clients with substance misuse issues, as well as assessing their needs, working on their personal action plans and referring them to any other appropriate services, should they need it

Project manager

You'll take day-to-day responsibility for the leadership and management of one of our projects, ensuring the delivery of a high quality service.

You'll also manage the service contracts and funding for the project, as well as identifying opportunities within the locality, to provide enhanced services for our clients.

Team leader

You'll provide day-to-day management support at the project and ensure that the service promised is the service delivered, as well as promoting both Addaction and the service itself.

This is just a selection of opportunities available. If you feel that you could contribute to our essential work, please get in touch. We'd love to hear from you.

→Addaction
t. 020 7017 2754
e. hr@addaction.org.uk
www.addaction.org.uk

FUNDRAISING MANAGER

Name: Karen Willis
Age: 27

So, what do you actually do? I lead fundraising throughout the North Bristol NHS Trust and am currently working towards the close of a £1.5 million appeal to refurbish the neonatal intensive care unit at Southmead Hospital.

How did you get into this job? I spent a year of my degree in Marketing and Business Management working for a large oil company and didn't exactly feel inspired monitoring the price of oil every day. I started doing lots of voluntary work in the evenings and decided that I should try and combine that with a job. I completed my degree and embarked on a career in fundraising. I worked for Cancer Research UK for three years and was looking for a new challenge where I could start something from scratch and watch it grow. This job came up just at the right time. And fundraising for the NHS certainly is a challenge.

What does your typical day involve? It can be anything from everyone buckling down together and stuffing envelopes to making pitches to corporates for Charity of the Year. Usually it starts with an essential cup of tea and a catch up with my team, followed by a juggling act of a variety of strategic fundraising activities, writing applications to charitable trusts, talking with supporters, and seeking out new opportunities.

What skills and experience do you need to work in this sector? You need to be highly organised with excellent communication skills. There are so many opportunities out there to raise money and you can't possibly do them all. You need to be able to select what you should be doing as an organisation and manage that effectively. You need to communicate your cause to the right audience in the right way. You need to stay innovative and push the boundaries.

What's the most challenging thing about the job? Communicating why we are fundraising for the NHS. So many people and organisations feel that we shouldn't have to fundraise for the NHS, but we are here to supplement the core funding and make the lives of the patients and their families easier.

What are your plans for the future? I'm very excited about the trust's next appeal. My ultimate ambition is to open an animal rescue centre – but that's a few years away yet. ▶

→**North Bristol NHS Trust**
t. 01179 753 753
e. tlc@nbt.nhs.uk
www.nbt.nhs.uk

MARKETING DIRECTOR

Name: Fiona Battle
Age: 3

So, what do you actually do? I'm responsible for making YouthNet, a national youth volunteering charity, a household name. I manage how the outside world perceives us. I'm also responsible for all our research activities and the profiling of our users.

How did you get into this job? I got a lucky break with my first marketing job. I applied for a position at ntl and got rejected, but when they were recruiting for a product manager they dug out my CV. Some people really do keep them on file! I then left ntl and went to work for Bloomberg. After Bloomberg, I worked for MTV.

After six years of working in the media, I felt that there must be more to life than pop stars. I decided to put my experience to better use, and moved to YouthNet. To get this job, I registered with a big marketing recruitment agency with a specialist charity team. I had a first interview, then prepared a presentation for my second interview. I 'clicked' with the CEO and got a real feel for YouthNet's creative atmosphere. How a place feels and its energy levels are really important to me.

What kind of personality is best suited to working in a job like yours? Within most organisations, the marketing team tends to play a very strategic role, so you need to be able to see and understand the big picture. You need to be a creative thinker who 'gets' popular culture. Networking – being a people person – is also crucial because you need to mix comfortably with all types. You've got to be brave and take some calculated risks because it's sometimes these ideas that create the best marketing campaigns.

What skills and experience do you need to work in this sector? I didn't really need any specific skills to move into the voluntary sector. I have, however, had to adapt my commercial experience and marketing techniques to suit. Charities tend to deal with a huge mix of stakeholders, so it helps to have an interest in, and understanding of, how other charities, opinion formers and policy makers work.

Best things about the job? Being given new opportunities all the time and the team that I work with. Also, really believing in what we do. That's so crucial. If you don't believe in the cause – and you're the 'voice' of the organisation – then nobody else will! ◗

→ **YouthNet**
t. 020 7226 8008
e. development@youthnet.org
www.youthnet.org.uk

WHO CARES WINS

Often poorly paid and poorly regarded, yet highly rewarding for those with a passion for helping some of the most vulnerable in society. **HUGH REILLY** introduces careers in social work and social care.

WHY WOULD anyone want to work in the social work or care sectors? Relentlessly negative national press coverage, long, often anti-social hours, layers of paperwork and bureaucracy, and the typically modest wage combine to make social care a seemingly thankless profession.

But 'thankless' is certainly not a word most social workers or carers would use to describe their job. For them, the reward gained from contributing to the wellbeing of disadvantaged members of society is unquantifiable.

"It's never dull," says Joanna Eggleton, senior care assistant at John Grooms care home for disabled people in Harrow, north London. "We're changing people's lives, and it changes your own life, it really does."

Although social care encompasses a huge range of different jobs – one in 20 of the adult working population work in care – at entry level, it is useful to make a distinction between social workers and social carers.

Social workers organise and help to provide the right kind of care for those who need extra support, such as homeless people, substance misusers, people with physical or learning difficulties, neglected children, people with mental health problems, or those whose lives have been affected by HIV/AIDS. Carers, meanwhile, provide the hands-on personal care that these groups need.

SOCIAL WORK

A rewardingly varied career, social work offers the opportunity to work with a wide range of people, and in a diverse range of locations:

a local council's social services; hospitals, trusts and GP practices; education departments and special schools; residential care homes and day centres; youth justice teams; drop-in centres and community projects.

As a social worker you might be visiting children in a care home to assess their health needs in the morning and making a home visit at lunchtime to ensure a disabled person has received the specialist equipment that has been ordered for them. Then in the afternoon you might meet an older person to help them claim benefits they are entitled to.

All social workers must be qualified – completing a recognised Social Work degree – and be registered as a social worker. To get onto the degree, a minimum of two A-levels or equivalent is the standard requirement, although the 61 UK universities which offer the course will all have their own specific entry requirements.

Mature students can also enter the degree course, providing they can demonstrate relevant experience. Graduates can complete the Social Work degree as a two-year post-graduate course which, according to Julie Wardle, senior careers advisor at the Social Care Careers Helpline, is proving an increasingly popular route.

"The main thing is to get relevant experience, whether it's just something with disabled kids or older people at the weekend," says Julie. "No matter what prior qualifications you have, all universities will ask for experience."

The helpline, which was set up by the Department of Health to increase recruitment in the sector, is a useful port of call for those considering a job in social work. It provides useful information on the bursaries available for those studying social work, which for many will cover at least the tuition fees.

Good places to find voluntary work vacancies include The Guardian on a Wednesday, and Community Care magazine – the social workers' weekly title. These publications also include unqualified social work vacancies, for roles such as support workers, care assistants and ancillary workers, which are excellent positions in which to gain the relevant pre-degree experience while still getting paid.

Many social work graduates get their first job in local government social services, which can pay as little as £14,000 per year, although in some areas of London, newly qualified social workers have been to known to earn as much as £28,000. There is also plenty of opportunity to gain automatic increments on your salary by taking on extra training and gaining seniority within the profession.

For many social workers, their first job in social services is a tough introduction into the world of social work. "It's definitely a baptism of fire," says Becca Einhorn, who began her career in a local authority social services department. "Prepare yourself for a great experience. I'm very glad I did my stint."

Becca, who started studying for her social

work qualifications at 39, demonstrates that age is not a barrier to entering social work. Although the minimum age for the new social work degree has been reduced to 18, most do not begin the course until their mid-20s, choosing instead to gain the life experience necessary for a career in this field.

A popular career path for social workers who become disillusioned by the sizeable quantity of paperwork that comes with the typically hefty social services caseload is the charity route. Becca now works for the children's charity NSPCC on a project that helps young girls who have been sexually abused.

"It's a more creative environment because it's much more groundbreaking with its particular projects," says Becca.

CARE WORK

Carers provide practical support for people with psychological or physical problems in a wide variety of locations, such as care homes and drop-in centres. A typical day for a carer might involve assisting a disabled person

to eat and go to the toilet, building up a relationship with a teenager in care by teaching them practical skills such as cooking, or helping someone with mental health problems sort out their domestic bills.

Unlike social work, you can become a carer without any academic qualifications. Increasingly, though, carers are being encouraged by the government to take the relevant care NVQs. which can be gained in the workplace.

"It might be that somebody shadows you or a supervisor might ask you questions about what you're doing and why you're doing it," says Joanna Eggleton, a senior care assistant at John Grooms in Harrow.

Although Joanna has been a carer in the private sector at an old people's home and with charities including Barnardos, she has only recently begun to study for her NVQ. "My advice would be to go for something that has the opportunity of doing an NVQ. If I could have done it earlier then I definitely would have," she says.

Among other care qualifications are the BTEC

national diploma in Health and Social Care, which school leavers can do to help gain employment as a support care worker. The agency, Skills for Care, also offers apprenticeships and diplomas in social care for 14-19 year-olds.

For many, as with social work, careers in care start with volunteering. "It is quite a leap going into this kind of work – you're working with vulnerable and damaged people who have a lot of support needs," says Nick Johnson, chief executive of the Social Care Association. "Volunteering with a caring organisation is the best way to see if the job is what you think it is." ▶

→**Social Care Careers Helpline**
www.socialcarecareers.co.uk

→**Community Care**
www.communitycare.co.uk

→**The Guardian**
http://society.guardian.co.uk

→**National Association of Volunteer Bureaux**
www.navb.org.uk

→**Community Service Volunteers**
www.csv.org.uk

HEALTH AND WELLBEING WORKER

Name: Skip Poppy
Age: 39

So, what do you actually do? I work as a counsellor and psychotherapist in a YWCA Young Women's Centre in Doncaster. The centre offers a range of support to empower young women to understand and exercise their own choices. I do both group work and one-to-one skills and therapy sessions. The range of issues we work on includes bullying, self-harm, rape, suicide, depression, addiction, relationship breakdown, and self-esteem. I also supervise and manage counsellors and project workers, as well as having responsibility for monitoring our work, networking with other agencies, and, like many others in this sector, doing any admin that is needed to support all these things.

Did you do any specific training or qualifications to get this job? Initially I was employed because of my counselling training and experience (an advanced diploma in Counselling). The YWCA supported me to complete a post-graduate diploma in Counselling Supervision and my psychotherapy training, both of which I use in my daily work.

How did you get into this job? Unintentionally – one step just led to the next. After college I worked for five years in the packaging industry. During my fourth year I decided I wanted to do something in my community. I saw an advert in a shop window looking to recruit volunteers for my local Rape Crisis Centre. I intended to do a couple of hours volunteering a week. I started volunteer work and realised that when I retired I didn't want to think: "Well, I contributed to the world having a lot of packaging." So, I volunteered again – this time for redundancy! I spent the next year working as a volunteer until I got a part-time paid post with the Rape Crisis Centre. This eventually led me to YWCA.

What are the most challenging things about your job? That it's never OK to have an 'off' day – I want to offer my full attention and skills to each person. It's the simple things, like really listening to everything a person says, staying alongside the client while encouraging and challenging them to move, and accepting when they aren't ready to.

Any top tips for someone wanting to get into this work? Go for it. Most of the things we regret are the things we never did. Get a good training with a reputable, accredited organisation, as mandatory regulation of the profession is on its way. ❯

➔**YWCA England & Wales**
t. 01865 304 200
e. info@ywca.org.uk
www.ywca-gb.org.uk

CARE SERVICE CO-ORDINATOR

Name: Kirsty Brown
Age: 28

So, what do you actually do? I ensure the smooth running of the Let's Go… service, which is part of a Scottish care charity called Momentum. We provide community-based activities and short breaks for adults with learning disabilities, helping them to increase their independence. I supervise and work alongside the support workers, plan breaks for service users, and make sure they receive the best possible support tailored to their individual needs.

What makes your job so ethical? We're assisting disabled and excluded people to achieve their goals. Let's Go… provides adults with learning disabilities with the opportunity to enjoy one-to-one support in the community and take part in activities that they choose, while actively promoting adult citizenship. The service we offer can be anything from going for a swim to a visit to the shops followed by a spot of lunch – it's very much led by the needs of the people who use it.

What kind of personality is best suited to working in a job like yours? You need to be a people person: outgoing, friendly, sensitive, patient, and a good listener with plenty of common sense. You need to be able to adapt to help the person you are supporting to help them feel at ease – everyone has a different personality.

What skills and experience do you need to work in this sector? Confidence in understanding the principles of caring about people is essential. Good communication skills are also required, as in addition to supporting people, you could be completing reports, liaising with other agencies and passing on vital information to them. It is important that your values and principles fit with present social policies and you have a genuine willingness to work with a range of people.

Best things about the job? Seeing real results. I'm involved in the initial referral process for Let's Go… so it's great to see someone six months down the line gaining confidence and independence, and building up a meaningful relationship with their support worker.

Any top tips for someone wanting to get into this work? Don't be put off if you haven't got the experience. Personal qualities are sometimes more important than qualifications: having the right heart and an aspiration to learn and succeed. Many organisations now support care staff to achieve qualifications. ▶

→**Momentum**
t. 0141 2 212 333
e. headoffice@
momentumscotland.org
www.momentumscotland.org

LOCAL ACTIVISM CO-ORDINATOR

Name: Raoul Bhambral
Age: 30

So, what do you actually do? I help to facilitate local activism among Friends of the Earth supporters, by working with campaign teams to organise effective and timely actions that can be taken by our local groups network. I meet with campaign teams to plan for local actions and advise on the expectations, capabilities and limitations of sections of our network, so that actions are designed to suit more than one type of local group.

What kind of personality is best suited to working in a job like yours? Someone who has the head space for more than one task at a time. I'm often quite busy, working on two or more campaigns on the go, as well as editing the local groups' magazine.

What skills and experience do you need to work in this sector? Key skills are patience, good time and task management, and the ability to get on with a wide range of people. A good working knowledge of how people function in groups is also essential.

What's the most memorable experience you've had in this job? Coming in one day, only to be immediately recruited as a pirate! We were holding an action outside a meeting of the International Maritime Organisation. I got to dress up, complete with parrot on one shoulder, and harass staff with my cutlass while roaring at them.

Best things about the job? Knowing that I'm helping over 200 groups of people take action on issues that concern them. Too often nowadays, people grumble about the state of the world without doing anything about it. The people I work for are actively involved in making our world a better place and I thrive on that.

What are your plans for the future? I'm keen to return to India and help set up a Friends of the Earth group there. At the moment, the various environmental movements in India are not connected. I'd really like to play a role in uniting them under one banner, bringing them in to the Friends of the Earth International network.

Any top tips for someone wanting to get into this work? The best way of getting into the voluntary sector is through volunteering yourself. That way you'll have a good understanding of what you, in turn, will ask of volunteers. You need lots of energy and a fearless approach to trying out new things. ❯

→**Friends of the Earth**
t. 020 7490 1555
e. info@foe.co.uk
www.foe.co.uk

ARTS AND CREATIVE

FAR FROM THE LUVVIE CROWD

GIDEON BURROWS meets Jamie Beddard, disabled theatre director and actor.

Photo: Jackie Chapman

JAMIE BEDDARD is an Actor. He is a writer. A Writer. Darling, he's a Director. Theatre and Film. He's worked with all the greats. Done the BBC you know. Lives in Islington. Writes a column. No, really. 'Jamie Beddard is unwell.' Magnificent!

When I met him in north London for our interview, Jamie Beddard was… unexpected. This theatre director is a self-confessed bit of a lad. But the 'unwell' of his column refers to his cerebral palsy, not to alcoholism brought on by the media luvvie lifestyle. Though you do get the impression that Beddard isn't afraid of knocking back a few beers.

The sidelines of Ipswich Town FC, rather than the back bar of the Groucho Club, is where you're likely to meet him. He lists his inspirations as Ska band Madness, and certainly doesn't take himself too seriously. Casting directors are warned on his CV that he walks funny and sounds odd. "Juggling will never be my forte," he includes under 'further skills'.

Maybe it's because Beddard fell into acting. For the former director of an award-winning theatre company, with BBC dramas and movies to his name, you'd expect there to have been some classical training. Even an interest in the arts?

"No, I just spent my time at Kent University doing what everyone else did – drinking and not doing much work. I had never acted before or even had the idea that I wanted to act."

But in 1995, the BBC put together a ground-breaking new screenplay, Scallagrigg – the first to feature actors with disabilities in real acting parts, rather than as oompa loompa extras. Back then, disabled actors weren't easy to come by.

"The BBC did a ring round of anyone who knew anyone, saying they needed someone with cerebral palsy. I had no idea I wanted to be involved in acting at that point. I went along to see them and told them how good I would be, and they believed me and gave me the job. I do feel guilty when I meet someone and they've been through three years of drama training."

As a theatre director, Beddard has been responsible for seeking out new talent, working with cutting-edge writers to perfect plays. Just occasionally, the lad takes a back seat, and the luvvie takes over.

"I love the creative side of the job. It's all about believability, and whether someone believes you or not is nothing to do with your disability. It was inspiring to be in Waiting for Godot, and it was a really big role. There's nothing like watching a play you've written being performed, or being there on the opening night as a director, and for it to go well. But writing is the most difficult, because you're on your own. In terms of creativity, I prefer to be with other people, and I'm not as disciplined as a writer as you need to be."

But if you catch him waxing lyrical in this way, and try to follow it up with a question about the inspiration behind his acting, why he finally chose it as a career, and the lad steps forward again:

"I got good money, and got well looked after. There was a world of opportunity – most of it debauched. I lived the life of an actor, which meant not working at all a lot of the time. And I got to meet Ian Dury, one of my heroes."

A hero? That must have been nice?

"Well, it was my first ever scene, and he was in it, raping me. Afterwards, though, he became a mate of mine."

Today, though, Beddard feels he's moved on from the debauched world of full-time acting, and the pay wasn't that good anyway. Now he prefers the creative side. On y occasionally does he land a screen or stage job, and goes "back to being a vacuous actor, and not care about the writing."

Working with disabled actors offers a particular challenge, necessarily giving the work an extra creative edge.

"When a disabled actor comes on stage, the audience immediately makes certain assumptions. The challenge is to make sure that by the time they've walked off the stage, the audience have been made to rethink that. Art is about difference and newness, and in a way disabled people are in a really good position because we have different bodies, and in the theatre or arts that s very exciting."

"I knew I was onto something when I got my first bad review," he says knowingly. "No cne ever gives disabled actors bad reviews. I've been terrible in a lot of my work, but I've not been judged by the same criteria."

So, at 38, what's next for this media lad, who's already top of his game in writing, directing and acting?

"Well, as an actor, you're always waiting for the phone to ring, but I am at that stage like all people of my age, always wondering where I'm going to be in 30 years time. The great thing about the world I'm in is that you never know what's going to happen next. I like that."

It is not as if the unexpected has done this accidental actor any harm in the past. ◗

This interview was originally carried out for the new website of **John Grooms**, a national disability charity.

→**John Grooms**
www.johngrooms.org.uk

ACTIVIST MEDIA PRODUCER

Name: Paul O'Connor
Age: 38

So, what do you actually do?

I work with Undercurrents to train people to produce videos highlighting non-violent activism within environmental and social issues, alongside producing programmes for the likes of the BBC and Channel 4. I also edit, operate professional digital video cameras, write articles for newspapers and magazines, do web design and co-produce the annual BeyondTV international video festival.

What makes your job so ethical?

We only work with groups who are aiming for positive social change. We oppose the arms trade and the traditional management structures of corporations. We involve many volunteers, strive to be as environmentally conscious as possible, and are determined to make films to bring about a change in the world.

How did you get into this job?

I started off by taking direct action to save trees from the chainsaw. I then began making activist videos, as well as filming and supplying images of protests to TV. I was a photographer from the age of 16 so moving into video wasn't that much of a learning curve. Spending two years on anti-road protests around the UK with a video camera gave me the best on-the-job training I could ask for. I learned to work in tricky, and sometimes dangerous, situations. Soon after, I met three like-minded people and we set up our own not-for-profit company, Undercurrents.

What's the most memorable experience you've had in this job?

Highlights include winning awards in Japan, France, Germany, UK, and the USA. It showed that people really are interested in the films I make. Seeing unarmed people shot dead by US or Israeli troops will stick with me for the rest of my life.

What are your plans for the future?

I'd like to produce my first feature film and follow in Michael Moore's footsteps.

Any top tips for someone wanting to get into this work?

Follow your heart rather than your head. Imagine yourself doing it and when the time comes, take a risk and jump! Don't stop and ponder for too long because you will talk yourself out of it. I abandoned my sales job at 25 and went travelling. From that trip I discovered how the world really is rather than how the media portrays it. ▶

→**Undercurrents**
t. 01992 455 900
e. info@undercurrents.org
www.undercurrents.org

EDITOR

Name: Cathryn Scott
Age 27

So, what do you actually do? As editor of The Big Issue Cymru and The Big Issue South West, I am responsible for researching material, arranging interviews and writing articles; commissioning other writers, photographers and illustrators; subbing other people's work; managing staff and budgets; and devising long-term editorial strategies, as well as many other things.

What makes your job so ethical? The Big Issue is a not-for-profit company that enables homeless people to move on in their lives by providing employment through selling a magazine. Also, the articles we write cover everything from human rights to environmental issues.

Did you do any specific training or qualifications to get this job? I did a post-graduate Journalism course at Cardiff, which teaches the specific skills needed, as well as plenty of work experience.

How did you get into this job? Through volunteer and freelance work with the magazine while I was a student. After four months, I was offered a part-time job and two months later went full time. Almost five years later, and I am the editor of two editions!

What skills and experience do you need to work in this sector? Generally, print journalists need to be educated to degree level and will often have studied Journalism at post-graduate level, on a course accredited by either the NCTJ or PTC. Good grammar and spelling skills are essential, as is a thirst for knowledge and an excellent understanding of the type of publication you want to work for. Being an editor is very different to being a journalist – management experience is a big help. For a magazine such as The Big Issue, you need a good knowledge of social issues affecting people in the UK.

Best things about the job? Knowing that every day you are making a difference to people's lives – from the vendors who sell the magazine to the people affected by the social injustices we campaign on. The free CDs and concert tickets are pretty good too!

Any top tips for someone wanting to get into this work? Get as much relevant work experience as you can. The industry is fiercely competitive. You won't be taken seriously unless you can demonstrate your commitment and experience in the field. Read anything and everything – it's one of the best ways of improving your writing. ❱

→**The Big Issue Cymru**
t. 02920 255 670
e. admin@bigissuecymru.co.uk
www.bigissuecymru.co.uk

CREATIVE LICENCE

The arts is not all about luvvies, champagne lunches and award ceremonies. As **JANE MORRIS** discovers, those of a creative persuasion can put their skills to use through working with communities too.

Photo: Orleans House Gallery

BEING AN artist, actor or musician has never looked like a particularly responsible career. Like many clichés, the romantic vision of the artist, either tortured and broke or spending their lives being harassed by the paparazzi, are at the two extremes of the scale.

In fact, there is also a much more practical face to this sometimes glamorous world. There are numerous artists, actors and musicians who use the arts as a way to improve the lives of vulnerable or disadvantaged people.

Councils and developers have begun to recognise the arts as an important element in urban regeneration projects. Thanks to increasing belief by the government in its power to "touch people's lives" as Tessa Jowell, the secretary of state for culture, puts it, more funding than ever is now being spent on what is sometimes called 'socially engaged' or 'community' art.

Much of the recent growth in community arts – and the resulting increase in career opportunities – is down to the National Lottery. The £19.5 million Urban Culture Programme, which will support a range of festivals, workshops, and arts initiatives over the next two years, is just one of several big-budget Lotto recipients within the community arts sector. Looking to the future, the London Olympic Games arts festivals leading up to 2012 are also expected to place an emphasis on the community.

Orleans House in Twickenham, West London, an 18th-century baroque mansion and classical art gallery, doesn't look like the sort of place to find much in the way of community art. But its curators have long been committed to working with disadvantaged young people. Their recent project, Inner Picture, worked with 25 young people from the local Hounslow Pupil Referral Service, which supports children who have been excluded from school, and the holiday scheme Positive Activities for Young People in nearby Richmond. Together with a group of artists, the 11–15 year-olds were asked to produce an exhibition based on how they felt others saw them.

Highlights included a 3D installation created by one of the young people, Josh Lindell. "I never thought I was any good at art," he says. "Actually I never thought I was good at anything. But I have proved to myself that I can do it."

Will Bishop Stephens is an animator who worked on Inner Picture. He studied sculpture at Winchester School of Art before opening a studio in Bristol, which he supported by doing "rubbish agency work, building work and the like". A few years ago he stepped in to fill a cancellation at Orleans House and hasn't looked back. He is currently working on his MA in Animation at the Royal College of Art.

"Working with young people is a very fruitful area," he says. "On this project, I thought the most direct way of working was for the kids to put themselves in the shoes of the characters in the portraits. The group devised their own scripts and we animated the portraits using their words." The children's work ended up on the walls of the National Portrait Gallery, hanging alongside the regular exhibitions by world-famous artists.

WHAT KIND OF JOBS ARE OUT THERE?

First, the good news: career prospects are on the increase. The flipside is that the previously rather amateur sector is also undergoing an increasing professionalisation. The biggest career division is between practitioners (such as musicians, artists and actors) and people who act as project managers, facilitators and educators. Artists typically go to art or drama school but may follow up with classes or even MAs in something like Community Arts or Education.

Sarah Carrington and Sophie Hope are a duo of socially engaged curators called B+B. They are artistic project managers who met while studying for a Masters in Curating in London. Their shared interest in art and society led them to create an independent agency to document and help initiate socially engaged art projects. They recently put together an exhibition called Real Estate about the ways in which artists and communities can work together to respond to, and effect, urban change.

"The art projects we showed ranged from artists training residents to use cameras to document the regeneration in their areas to creating an archive of 'local heroes', selected by residents at a time when the community was undergoing rapid change," says Sophie. "The exhibition demonstrated that artists can invent and share with local people new ways of expressing their views about the urban regeneration often being imposed around them."

WHERE DO YOU WORK?

Most commonly, people working in this kind of creative and cultural engagement are self employed, acting as consultants or contractors to particular projects. There is also a wealth of posts among community arts organisations, and specially created community and education-related posts in museums, galleries and theatres. Increasingly, even local authorities are employing their own community-based artists and musicians.

WHAT KIND OF TRAINING DO YOU NEED?

There are many ways into the sector, but arts training, education or social work are common entry routes. A degree, a postgraduate qualification and work experience are very useful, although some people do come up through grass roots organisations.

Annette McCartney works as education and events manager at London Transport Museum. She recently worked on a project that brought together black performance poet Abe Gibson and the museum's historic archive of black London Transport workers. He created a series of poems, including one based on 'Jamaican Joe', London's first black bus driver. He used this to develop workshops with the black community of Tottenham, where Joe lived, researching existing family members and even inspiring a regular reading group at the Marcus Garvey library.

McCartney fell into this kind of work almost by accident, after a BA in

Archaeology, and an MA in Museum Studies at Leicester University (which has a strong social element in all its cultural courses). "You need to be flexible," she says, "and you need a considerable mixture of skills: interest in people, good communication, able to deal with people who can be difficult. You also tend to end up running projects almost single handed, so you have to be able to fundraise, budget, and assess programmes. It is very hard work but also very rewarding."

There are some university courses specifically related to community arts. Goldsmiths College at the University of London offers a Masters in Theatre Education, while the University of York similarly offers a Masters in Community Music. The situation is less formalised in the visual arts world, although Dartington College in Devon has included community working in all its creative courses for years. Other people come with a degree or postgraduate study in Arts Management, or have a PGCE or similar in Education.

WHAT SORT OF SALARIES CAN YOU EXPECT?
The sector is competitive and generally not well paid. Freelance rates vary from £100 to £250 a day, although the new Arts Council minimum is £175 for most practitioners. But as a freelance, don't forget you'll need to account for holidays, sickness and down time when you won't get paid.

Entry-level salaries in employed posts are around £16,000, although a recent Museums Association salary survey found starting salaries for museum and gallery education officers were as low as £14,000. Salaries for people with some years' experience range from around £22,000 to £28,000. ▶

→**Arts Council England**
www.artscouncil.org.uk

→**Museums, Libraries and Arts Council**
www.mla.org.uk

→**Theatre Education Network**
www.theatre-ed.net

→**Foundation for Community Dance**
www.communitydance.org.uk

COMMUNITY INVOLVEMENT MANAGER

Name: Ali Orman
Age: 41

So, what do you actually do? I'm responsible for prostate cancer awareness-raising programmes for members of African-Caribbean communities, for the Prostate Cancer Charity. I also identify and provide culturally appropriate and culturally sensitive support.

What makes your job so ethical? I am helping a group of men that are not always prioritised by the health system and need help to make sure that their needs are heard. I make sure that this group of men are aware of prostate cancer.

What does your typical day involve? I spend most of my time out in one of the five regions I'm responsible for. There, I meet with health advisory groups and help them plan new initiatives that they are putting together in their communities. I may also do a local radio interview or write a visit report during my travelling time.

What kind of personality is best suited to working in a job like yours? You need to be outgoing, hardworking, unafraid of a challenge, and sensitive to the needs of others. You also need to be the kind of person that doesn't give up easily.

What skills and experience do you need to work in this sector? You need to have a heightened awareness of issues facing socially excluded and stigmatised communities. You need to have been instrumental in setting up and providing frontline services for a number of black and minority ethnic communities in terms of health promotion and health care.

What's the most memorable experience you've had in this job? The launch of the Prostate Cancer Information for African-Caribbean Men leaflet, which took place in Liverpool with former England footballing star, John Barnes. The day was a great success with more than 800 African-Caribbean men, women and children attending the event.

What are your plans for the future? World domination! Failing that, for our African-Caribbean Awareness Project to be rolled out nationally, and for every man to be aware of prostate cancer.

Any top tips for someone wanting to get into this work? Don't do it if you're not prepared to work hard. Speak to people in the sector and try and get some work experience. ▶

→**The Prostate Cancer Charity**
t. 020 8222 7622
e. info@prostate-cancer.org.uk
www.prostate-cancer.org.uk

MUSICIAN

Name: Charlotte Walls
Age: 27

So, what do you actually do? I'm a flutist with the charity Live Music Now. We perform to any audience that cannot get to a live performance. These include special needs schools, day care centres, residential homes, hospitals and hospices.

What makes your job so ethical? We're going to people who wouldn't otherwise experience live music, and we're giving them the opportunity to enjoy that music on their own terms. When you watch a performance on stage, you are somehow separated from it, viewing it from the outside. Taking the performance to someone means that we can tailor it to suit them, and they can become as involved as they wish.

How did you get into this job? I had always been aware of Live Music Now through college. We formed a group with the purpose of auditioning to be on the scheme. We were fascinated by the work, auditioned and were accepted.

What kind of personality is best suited to working in a job like yours? You need to be completely uninhibited, happy to make a fool of yourself and express yourself, especially when working with children with learning disabilities. You need to be open and outgoing and get on with people. You need to be compassionate and sincere, and care about what you are doing.

What skills and experience do you need to work in this sector? Obviously you need to be trained in music. Live Music Now employs musicians who are trained in a variety of musical genres. You need to be bright enough to think on your feet and bothered enough to think about your audience.

What's the most memorable experience you've had in this job? I remember doing a concert in a day centre for older people. One gentleman said he had played the flute before, but because he couldn't play it any more he became quite emotional. We kept the performance happy and light, but let him express himself. We found out later that no-one in the centre had heard him speak before. On a brighter note, we've had kids who have got up and danced – we had a kid of about 11 who started breakdancing!

Best things about the job? The experiences you have, the people you meet, the opportunity to get a sincere, immediate response from your audience – making them laugh or smile and bringing something different into their lives. ❿

→ **Live Music Now**
t. 020 7493 3443
e. auditions@livemusicnow.org
www.livemusicnow.org

MAKING PLACES WORK

Careers in regeneration and sustainable communities

A special supplement supported by:

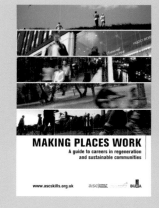

MAKING PLACES WORK
A guide to careers in regeneration
and sustainable communities

www.ascskills.org.uk

It's great when you visit a place that is different, attractive and lively. Unfortunately not everywhere is like that. If you're already in the business of developing communities then you know how to turn things around. You know how to make a community work. The problem is that you're a rare breed. The Academy for Sustainable Communities (ASC) aims to ensure there are enough people, with the right skills to sustain prosperous and attractive communities across the country. From bricks and economics to child care and conservation, you can develop your skills and learn how to make a real difference to the way we live. Get involved, get moving, get in touch. Visit somewhere new, **visit www.ascskills.org.uk**

asc | **Academy for Sustainable Communities**

INTRODUCTION

WELCOME to Making Places Work, a special supplement on working in regeneration and sustainable communities.

Wherever you are reading this guide, you will be part of a community. Perhaps you're in a bustling city centre or a peaceful country town, maybe a modern housing development or a traditional, scenic village. You might be in a school, a university, a library or a careers centre. Whatever your community, it will have its own individual characteristics.

Creating these different communities and making sure that they continue to meet the needs of those who live, work, study or play in them involves a wide range of professions. This guide has been created to give you an insight into these exciting and rewarding careers, all of which allow you to help transform local places, tackle the problems of our day and make a real difference to the lives of many people.

Over these pages we'll explain exactly what is meant by a 'sustainable community' and 'regeneration'. The guide highlights the kind of careers that are out there for those who care about the world around them, and provides a wealth of information on how to take those first steps to landing a career that truly matters.

The Academy for Sustainable Communities is proud to be involved with this guide. Whether your ambition is to help deliver the Olympic facilities in east London or run a sports centre for community groups in Liverpool, carry out voluntary youth work in your home town or become an internationally renowned architect, read on to learn more about how you can become part of the future.

At the back, there's a directory of organisations that will point you in the right direction. You can also register at our website to be kept up to date. Good luck!

GILL TAYLOR
Chief Executive

asc | Academy for Sustainable Communities

www.ascskills.org.uk

COMMUNITY SPIRIT

There are a range of careers involved in making communities better for the long term. ADRIAN SANDIFORD offers an overview.

IN the UK, a person's life chances – their health, job prospects and life expectancy – still very much depend on their postcode. This may be one of the wealthiest nations on the planet, but behind the shine there are vast areas that have fallen into a cycle of decline and neglect.

These are what politicians like to call 'deprived communities'. Whole estates, even towns, are facing a multitude of issues like low employment, poor health, substance misuse, and high truancy rates. The truth is that

certain neighbourhoods just don't work.

Yet, things are slowly changing for the better. By developing a career in sustainable communities, you can be part of the transformation.

Sustainable communities is all about turning neighbourhoods around, for good. Whether a newly built housing or business project, or the regeneration of a former rundown area, making a community sustainable takes more than just modern bricks or a new park.

It's about ensuring the community will continue

to prosper long after the builders have packed up. That means fully involving the community in its own future. It means ensuring that a neighbourhood gets what the area really needs, not just what looks pretty or fits a funding stream. Without these vital elements, any project faces being just another rundown chunk of bricks and road within a decade.

A strong community is one with positive community spirit, good local services and shops, a safe and healthy local environment, long-term employment and lasting opportunities.

"The point of sustainable communites is to address the different elements that affect people's quality of life: social, physical, economic, environmental, and cultural," says Jess Steele, deputy chief executive of the British Urban Regeneration Association (BURA).

With these things, a community shouldn't need future outside interventions. It becomes sustainable.

But turning an area around to a point where it can sustain itself is a huge task. It depends on people from various professions working together. For a community to 'work', everything from the physical layout of an area to the type of shops and services available, and the number

and type of local businesses, has to be developed. The people who make it happen include architects, local government officers, planners, community leaders, youth workers and accountants. Whatever your background there's a career for you helping to make communities work better.

"We're all members of the same team," says Professor Peter Roberts, chair of the Academy for Sustainable Communities. "There may be different roles but we all have a common goal."

And if you're currently working in business, local government or for a charity, your knowledge and skills will be very welcome.

"Most people come into the sector from a different field, becoming interested

in sustainable communities through a specific area and project," says Steele. "The most important thing is that you're in it for the right reason, a motivation to improve the quality of life for communities."

GRANGE PARK COMMUNITY PROJECT, BLACKPOOL

Grange Park was one of the most deprived estates in the country. A community of 1,800 households faced anti-social behaviour, poor diet and low employment. But in 1997, Blackpool Borough Council launched the Grange Park Community Project, bringing specialist groups, council departments, businesses and residents into partnership to find ways to improve quality of life.

Community at Heart, Bristol: engaging the whole community

"Things became more focused and we could do things for the community that people wanted and needed," says Peter Jefferson, the project's assistant director of landlord services. "There was an expectation that together something was going to happen."

And it did. The project's achievements include tenants working closely with architects to redesign buildings, and the establishment of a City Learning Centre on the estate, with library, IT suite and TV training studio. There's a new primary school and there's a new healthy eating café. Each of these has been put in place because local residents thought it would help develop their community for the better.

COMMUNITY AT HEART, BRISTOL

This community-led partnership was given £50 million to regenerate an inner-city area of 6,000 people living in 3,200 households. Residents are involved and consulted on all work, electing over half the management board. Three years later, the partnership is running 120 projects.

"What I really like is that we're dealing with all the issues at the same time," says chief executive, David Ralph. "We're bringing all the strategies together and there's active involvement from the residents."

"If you're going to go into this field, you need two vital abilities. One is an interest in community development and working with residents. The other is a specialisation, whether it's crime reduction, health or management."

CPR URBAN REGENERATION COMPANY, CORNWALL

Sustainable communities are not just about inner cities. The Camborne, Pool and Redruth Urban Regeneration Company is driving a £150 million investment programme in west Cornwall, bringing together public funding from bodies like English Partnerships and the South West Regional Development Agency.

Their plan includes 15 key projects to be delivered over five years, creating an estimated 2,500 jobs, over 940 high-quality homes, and in excess of 20,000 square metres of industrial premises.

"We're acting as facilitators," says the project's urban design manager, Tim Kellet. "Our key role is to set standards, work out what needs to be done, and bring people to the table who can deliver." ∎

Blackpool Borough Council
www.blackpool.gov.uk

Community at Heart
www.ndcbristol.co.uk

CPR Urban Regeneration Company
www.cprregeneration.co.uk

BURA
www.bura.org.uk

SO, WHAT DO YOU DO?

You're flicking through the job pages, ready to launch your career. But what does that job title actually mean? Join us on a jargon-busting journey through the classifieds.

PARTNERSHIP OFFICER You're the people person. Projects require lots of different partners to work together. Rather like Christmas dinner, you'll make sure everyone stays friends and are working towards the same aim. You'll also ensure various plans fit together.

COMMUNITY ENGAGEMENT MANAGER A project is nothing without the people it's supposed to help. You'll reach out to residents, get and keep everybody on board.

EMPLOYMENT AND TRAINING MANAGER Regeneration isn't just about buildings and business, it's about people. This managerial role focuses on maximising the employment, training and business opportunities for people living in neighbourhoods.

COMMUNITY SAFETY CO-ORDINATOR Think crime-fighter, but without the cape. This job is all about developing fresh approaches to crime reduction, bringing different players and communities together.

REGENERATION PROJECT MANAGER This won't be your first job. To co-ordinate all stages of a project from its inception to completion requires years of experience, superb leadership and management skills, and an understanding of the different people needed to make things work.

BUSINESS DEVELOPMENT OFFICER An area's economy is key to its success. Good marketing, financial planning and strategy are all needed. You'll support local businesses to get the assistance they need, from professionals who can help.

ENGINEER Involved in the structural side of regeneration, with responsibility for the technical aspects of construction work, from securing materials to supervising sub-contractors.

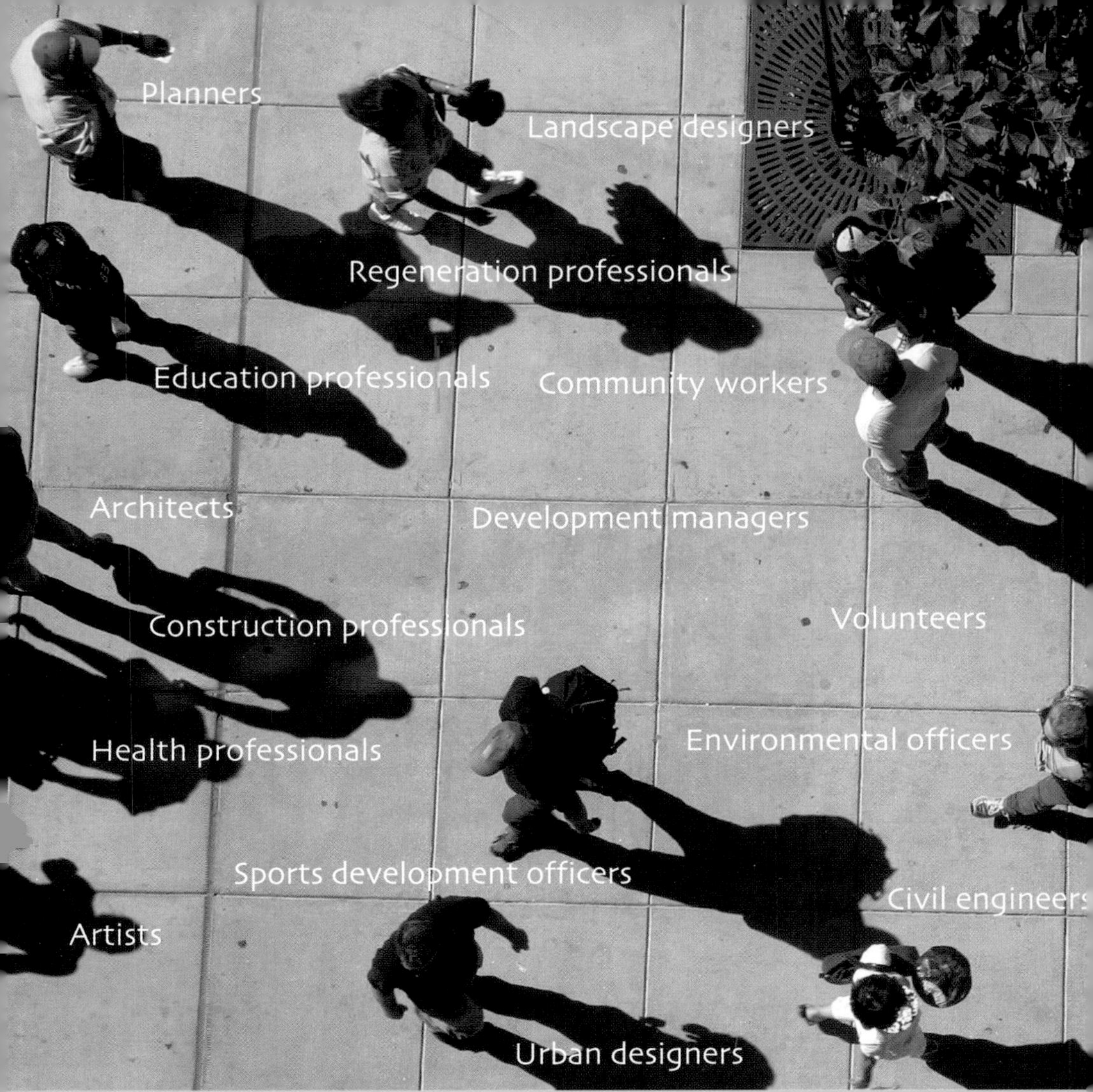

Planners
Landscape designers
Regeneration professionals
Education professionals   Community workers
Architects   Development managers
Construction professionals   Volunteers
Health professionals   Environmental officers
Sports development officers
Civil engineers
Artists
Urban designers

Planning, delivering and maintaining sustainable communities - places where people can live, work, and enjoy their lives - requires over 100 occupations to work together, from development workers and police to planners and teachers.

Creating:excellence is at the heart of sustainable community development in South West England, facilitating the spread of knowledge, experience and ideas between people involved in making regeneration and renewal happen. We want you to get involved in this rewarding work - visit www.creatingexcellence.org.uk for more information.

creating:excellence
the south west centre for sustainable communities

Name Max Woodford

Age 29

ECONOMIC DEVELOPMENT OFFICER

So, what do you actually do?
I project manage medium-to-large-scale physical regeneration projects for Brighton & Hove City Council. This involves writing development briefs, selecting who is going to carry out the work, assisting our planning department and arranging community consultation.

How does it fit into sustainable communities?
The work is all about physical regeneration, but we also need to ensure the finished site is sustainable in environmental and community terms. Often the sites are in areas of high deprivation, so regeneration has to tie in with local needs, rather than just 'dropping in' a lot of expensive flats.

How did you get into this job?
I got a degree in Politics from the University of Sussex, and a Masters in Town Planning. I got a part-time temporary post working for the planning enforcement team as a result of writing in to ask for work experience. From there I became a planning enforcement officer, a planning officer and the planning enforcement team leader. I saw this job on the internal list of vacancies.

What kind of personality is best suited to working in a job like yours?
You need to be a pragmatist. You also need to be able to maintain good working relationships with people from a variety of sectors, be it residents from very deprived housing estates or the global property directors of major corporations.

What skills and experience do you need to work in this sector?
Knowledge of the built environment and the development process helps. You need to be able to negotiate, and have the ability to spot a problem, keep it in perspective, and think up ways of working around it.

Best things about the job?
Seeing vacant sites move back towards beneficial use, the variety of tasks, and generally working in the built environment sector.

Any top tips for someone wanting to get into this work?
Be proactive about trying to seek out work experience – I got my first job out of it. At the very least, see if you can talk to people working in the field you are interested in. ■

Brighton & Hove City Council
t. 01273 291 119
e. regenerating@ brighton-hove.gov.uk
www.brighton-hove.gov.uk

BRIGHT SPARKS

Open spaces: Hemingway Design aims to link affordability, environment and inspiration

When it comes to creating sustainable communities, an outgoing personality can make all the difference. PAUL ALLEN meets three people who have been at the heart of inspiring community-based projects.

DESIGN FOR LIFE

Wayne Hemingway made his name in the late 1980s as the charismatic co-founder of fashion label Red or Dead. But when he and wife Gerardine sold the company in 1999, they travelled the world and discovered a new passion – social housing. In almost every foreign country they found examples of exciting new housing estates. Back home it was a very different picture.

Shocked by reports that only 28 percent of the housebuying population would consider moving into a new built property, Wayne wrote an angry article in the national press criticising modern-day property developers for being more concerned about making profits than vibrant, sustainable communities. In response, George Wimpey invited him to work on a series of luxury penthouses,

but Wayne insisted on designing affordable housing.

"I can understand why they thought a designer would want to work on fancy riverside apartments, but that didn't interest me," he says. "I grew up on a fantastic estate in Blackburn and I wanted to show that it was possible to create high quality, mass-market housing."

The result was the Staiths South Bank, an 800-property project in a deprived area of Tyneside. Its designs included several different kinds of homes, from townhouses to apartments, using a variety of layouts and building materials. There were other innovations too. Roads were narrower, with wider pavements and a bias towards the pedestrian. Wayne also created a range of shared green spaces.

"A big problem on estates today comes from youth crime, but if you get kids to enjoy where they live, they won't want to destroy it."

In 2005, Staiths South Bank won Building magazine's 'Best Housing-Led Regeneration Project'.

"I don't think we've ever felt so excited or proud about anything," says Wayne.

CHANGING FACES

In the early 1990s, the Beacon and Old Hill estate in Cornwall was one of the UK's most deprived areas. Nicknamed 'Beirut' by locals, the drab rows of run-down, low-rise terrace houses were rife with social problems. More than half the homes lacked central heating, eight out of ten local men were unemployed, crime was endemic. In 1995, two visiting health workers called a meeting to address worrying levels of childhood asthma and post-natal depression. Only Grenville Chappel and his wife came.

Grenville, a former navy man, was born on the estate in 1948. He recalls Old Hill as a friendly, inclusive neighbourhood. But when he returned in the late 1980s after a 20-year absence, that sense of community spirit had disappeared. "There were all sorts of problems," he says. "And people didn't believe it was going to get better – they'd heard too many promises before."

Grenville's leadership experience gave him the confidence to front the residents' fight back. Reinstating a sense of local pride was his chief motivation.

In 1995, Grenville became chairman of the new residents' association, which became part of the Beacon Community Regeneration Partnership (BCRP). Two years later, he helped BCRP apply for a successful £1.2 million grant bid to improve infrastructure on the estate.

"It was a massive responsibility," says Grenville, now project co-ordinator, "especially when everyone was saying they needed the money most."

After improving home insulation on the estate, Grenville's team began to address the wider environment. Local people were asking for traffic-calming measures, and when their concerns were acted on, a new sense of trust began to grow.

"People realised that we were actually getting things done. They saw that we, as local residents, were listening and they began to believe in us."

Since then, there have been numerous improvements: from new doors and lighting to a skateboard park, youth groups and a community centre. Meanwhile, crime in the area has more than halved.

Independent Photography: socially engaged art projects

In 2003, the project collected a Queen's Jubilee Award and Deputy Prime Minister's award for sustainable communities.

"People now have a new respect for the estate," Grenville says. "Now there are people from all over the country who are applying to live here."

ART MATTERS

"People get involved in our projects for all sorts of reasons," says Isabel Lilly, artistic director of south London-based Independent Photography. "One of the most important things is simply to bring them all together."

The company specialises in socially engaged art – creating and promoting art projects within local communities. They engage local residents to explore the issues that matter to them most.

Isabel began her career in community education, and after training as a photographer, started running photography courses for unemployed people. There has always been a strong social dimension to her work.

"I had always been working with different people within the community," she says. "The move into socially engaged art seemed like a very logical step."

In summer 2002, Isabel approached local estates in Greenwich. From their meetings, she began Imagine East Greenwich (IEG), a series of eight community art projects that encompassed a broad range of artistic media: from film to writing, graphic design to music.

The final programme reflected local people's concerns: a website design initiative for young people about drug awareness, a creative writing scheme for children, and a film and photography workshop for young women to explore health issues.

"Health Matters, the project, gave the women a space to talk about difficult issues, such as domestic violence, which many of them hadn't had before," says Isabel.

Isabel is now involved in phase two of IEG, which focuses on mental health issues on the estate.

"This area is set to see vast changes over the next decade," she says. "Our projects are starting to involve people in these issues at an early stage." ■

Hemingway Design
www.hemingwaydesign.co.uk

The Beacon Community Regeneration Project
www.bcrp.carrick.gov.uk

Independent Photography
www.independentphotography.org.uk

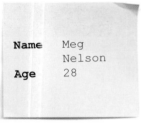

Name Meg
Nelson

Age 28

PLANNER

So, what do you actually do? 'm assistant planner at GVA Grimley, a property and planning consultancy. I advise landowners and developers on achieving planning consent for their development projects, as well as on other planning issues. In particu ar, I work on retail, residential and major mixed-use development schemes.

How does it fit into sustainable communities? Planning is very much about 'place making': creating safe, sustainable communities that will be successful now and in the future. Any development project contributes towards this process. One example is our work on the redevelopment of Leith Docks 'n north Edinburgh. The Development Framework will now guide the future redevelopment of 170 hectares cf dockland for up to 18,000 homes, creating a new, sustainable waterfront community.

What does your typical day involve? Every day is a busy day. Core activities are making planning applications, research, policy review and site appraisal. This involves site visits, meetings with clients, councils and public consultation. On the larger jobs I'll be working with other professions, mainly architects, u ban designers and transport consultants.

How did you get into this job? My dad suggested the idea of town planning to me four years ago when I was looking for an interesting job to put my mind to. I did the MSc Urban and Regional Planning course at Heriot-Watt University, over two years full time. After summer work experience at West Lothian Council in strategic planning, I also did work experience for GVA Grimley, which turned into a full-time job with them.

What skills and experience do you need to work in this sector? People skills, an interest in buildings and how urban spaces work, knowledge of the planning system, and lots of energy.

Best things about the job? Variety – planning is such a broad field, involving design, law, economics and the environment. The maps I have to work with are cool too. ∎

GVA Grimley (Edinburgh)
t. 0870 900 89 90
e. enquiries@gvagrimley.co.uk
www.gvagrimley.co.uk

Solent Centre: shaping the future of Southampton

GOING LOCAL

Working in sustainable communities means you'll be mixing the 'bricks and mortar' of building and renovation projects with softer community-based work. ELEANOR STANLEY meets those already uniting the two.

FOR many years, the former mining community of Pendeen, on the rugged west Cornish coast, has been the scene of severe deprivation.

It has poor transport links, high levels of unemployment and little for young people to do. But four years ago a pioneering regeneration project brought together members of the local community to do something for themselves to improve their local area: they decided to renovate a ramshackle snooker and pool hall.

Today, the building is home to an award-winning, state-of-the-art community space called the Centre of Pendeen. It offers a rich programme of training, youth groups, sports facilities and social events, bringing life back to the community.

This scheme is just one example of how communities can be revitalised and given a sustainable future. Regeneration needs a mix of 'hard' interventions, such as the design, construction and physical building or renovation of areas, and the 'softer' side of working to engage and involve the local community, charities and voluntary groups, to find out what local people's needs are, and to find ways to meet them.

"A lot of mistakes have been made in the past, when ideas of how communities could be planned and built were imposed on people by architects, planners and politicians," explains Bruce Macveen, policy adviser at the Commission for Architecture and the Built Environment. "Today, professionals involved in regeneration are realising that their role is to support and facilitate local communities in identifying problems, and the solutions to those problems."

Peter Holbrooke, 34, is director of the Sunlight Development Trust, a community project run from a renovated laundry, in Gillingham, Kent. Peter studied Environmental Management, but worked in retail and then marketing, including a stint at Oxfam, before returning to his home town. There he set up a successful initiative, which offers a range of community facilities and activities.

"The built element is only part of what we've done," he says. "To truly regenerate an area, the social has to happen alongside the physical. Education and experience helps, you need empathy and a passion for what you're doing. Some see community participation as a burden, I see it as a great privilege."

Billy Davis, 14, is just one of the young people for whom the Sunlight Centre has been life changing: "I got kicked out of school, so I started coming to the project because there was nothing else to do. I helped choose the colours, and design a sign. They gave us a wall to graffiti. Now I'm helping to build a new radio station."

Mark Drury is director for arts and education at the Solent Centre for Architecture and Design, a new organisation promoting design that achieves environmental and social sustainability. "This area of work is as wide as you want it to be," he says. "We want to bring in people from different career paths. For example, working on the difficulties of vandalism might involve street lighting teams, crime prevention officers and the police, as well as architects and planners."

Many of the people

The Sunlight Centre: social regeneration alongside the physical

working in this field have a strong sense of social justice and a desire to engineer a change. For job seekers, the advantage of the community-based emphasis is that there are plenty of opportunities to gain work experience, by getting involved in local groups.

Joel Parkes, 26, studied Design and Public Art before doing a training course at Freeform – an arts-led community regeneration charity. Now he works there as an assistant project manager, co-ordinating everything from redesigning parks to designing sculptures for local estates.

"We run creative workshops with local people to get input and ideas for local design. The process is just as important as the end product. It's the opposite of coming in and plonking things in their communities – people like to be listened to. My job is trying to get people to yield something that they'll be happy with. There's a strong sense of fulfilment."

But working with communities isn't always easy – it can mean finding solutions to conflicting views and finding ways to meet demands that are difficult to implement. Catherine Prasad, 31, a project manager for the National Trust, studied Environmental Science. She found that community participation has been a key aspect of her work throughout her career.

"It can be quite challenging – you've got to be prepared to take a lot of flak," she says. "If someone complains, I always think that's a positive sign – people feel they can shape where they live, and that has to be empowering."

Saira Ali, 35, is a landscape architect working for City of Bradford Metropolitan District Council. After her art foundation course, she studied Landscape Architecture and worked in private practice around the country before starting her current job. She says working with her own community is the most inspiring aspect of the job.

"I came back to Bradford because it's my home and I wanted to play a part, however small, in the rejuvenation of the city. I enjoy talking to people about what they want and then being able to deliver on the practical side. I can take the vision of the community and the team I work with, and make it a reality. I want the communities who I work with to feel proud when they say 'This is where I live.'"

Back in Pendeen, the centre has won the RegenSW renewable energy agency's green award for the best community scheme.

"It is a fantastic building," says centre manager Tracey Waters. "But it's much more than that. Our building is a centre for the Pendeen community. The community spirit is very, very strong, and everyone has really pulled together to find the right solution." ■

CABE
www.cabe.org.uk

Centre of Pendeen
www.centreofpendeen.co.uk

Solent Centre
www.solentcentre.org.uk

Sunlight Development Trust
www.sunlighttrust.org.uk

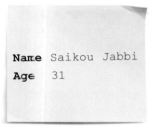

Name Saikou Jabbi
Age 31

COMMUNITY WARDEN

So, what do you actually do? I work for Hull Community Wardens, part of the Goodwin Development Trust. I help asylum seekers settle into the area, introduce them to various agencies and support them in their new community. I address school assemblies to help young people understand what seeking asylum is about, encouraging young people to get to know those from other countries. As a community warden, I also do regular patrols, providing reassurance and acting as the 'eyes and ears' of the community.

How does it fit into sustainable communities? My job is about generating good community relationships, helping people to understand diversity or integrate into new surroundings. By introducing and developing cultural programmes, we're bringing people from various countries and backgrounds together to foster a better understanding of different cultures.

What kind of personality is best suited to a job like yours? Because the work is diverse, you have to be prepared to accept anything. You need to be patient, understanding, a good listener as well as a good communicator. You must be impartial and have the passion to make a difference.

Best things about the job? Being recognised for doing my job well by residents, colleagues, agencies, and my employer. It is gratifying to know that the work I do changes people's lives for the better.

What's the most memorable experience you've had in this job? At the 2004 National Wardens' Conference, I was given an award from the Office of the Deputy Prime Minister for my work with diversity issues, which made me very proud and humble. The other memorable experience is somewhat darker: I had to arrange for the burial of two asylum seekers who had passed away. These people had absolutely no one. It was a life-changing experience for me.

What are your plans for the future? I want to keep on doing more of what I already do: promoting cohesion and inclusion, organising events to maintain the profile of what I do, and, ultimately, help people. ■

Goodwin Development Trust
t. 01482 587 550
e. info@goodwin-centre.org
www.goodwin-centre.org

Name	Stephen Slocombe
Age	47

DEVELOPMENT MANAGER

So what do you actually do? I promote Newport Unlimited, the first Urban Regeneration Company in Wales, through presentations to private-sector developers, negotiation and management of joint ventures with public and private sector bodies, and project management.

How did you get into this job? I left school with A-levels and worked in banking for eight years. When I was 27 I decided to go back to full-time education, obtained a BSc in Urban Estate Management and then became a Member of the Royal Society of Chartered Surveyors.

I began working for the Welsh Development Agency as a regional property surveyor. I moved into property development and then into an urban regeneration role as an Urban Development Manager, and after that I moved to Newport Unlimited.

What kind of personality is best suited to working in a job like yours? An outgoing personality is essential. A dogged determination is also required coupled with a positive outlook. It's too easy to be negative about things. The ability to interact across a broad spectrum of professions and personalities is also important, as there are so many organisations involved in the regeneration process.

What skills and experience do you need to work in this sector? I've learnt all the skills required for the job through work experience.

Best things about the job? The satisfaction of turning a hopeless cause into a success combined with the unpredictability of the job, the variety of the work and the people. The regeneration process never stops – it's a sustainable career.

Worst things about the job? The most challenging aspect of the job is not to be thrown off course by adversity. You need to remain focused and determined to get things done even when you don't feel like it.

Any top tips for someone wanting to get into this work? Get a relevant professional qualification. Be prepared to learn something new every working day. Get stuck in and get your hands dirty. Don't be diverted by negativity. ∎

Newport Unlimited
t. 01633 844 141
e. info@newportunlimited.co.uk
www.newportunlimited.co.uk

NEXT STEPS

KATIE TOMS offers advice on some key career routes into the sustainable communities sector.

THERE has never been a better time to begin a career working in the sustainable communities sector.

For a start, people with the right background or experience are in huge demand. In 2004, a government-backed inquiry revealed massive skills shortages in everything from architecture and the arts to community liaison and construction. It's a rapidly growing sector. That means job prospects are great, and career development opportunities very optimistic.

And the vast range of jobs falling under the sustainable communities umbrella means whatever your interests or skills, there is a place for you.

"The great thing about this sector is that projects are fairly short term, so there's lots of opportunity to move around geographically and career wise," explains Dave Boardman at the University of Bradford's School of Lifelong Education and Development.

Vitally, if you have passion and enthusiasm for working with people and care about communities, then the personal rewards are immense.

"Regeneration, if it's done properly, is about putting hope back into individuals and communities," says Boardman. "If that doesn't reward you, you should go and work in a bank."

So if you've got big ideas for your career, here's how to go about it.

THE ACADEMIC APPROACH

Practically any degree will give you a good start in the sector, though some jobs such as construction or engineering are likely to need

something more specific. For planning or architecture, you'll also need to study for a professional qualification in the field.

But the sector has become so recognised now that you can actually study Sustainable Communities or Regeneration as academic disciplines themselves.

Boardman says even a job in the sector cannot offer the breadth of understanding gained from a degree. "It is important to have some understanding of issues across the board. Few people in regeneration have studied what regeneration is about, its context and how it all fits together."

Bradford offers a foundation degree in Community Regeneration and Development and Liverpool a degree in Urban Regeneration and Planning.

For a more extensive list, see the resources directory on page 82.

WORK EXPERIENCE

Whether you have a qualification or not, work experience can be the key to unlocking doors. Hazel Egan is co-ordinator of the volunteering programme at environmental regeneration charity Groundwork. She started out as a volunteer on the scheme.

"Graduates have proven academically that they know the subject matter, but they often don't have the experience to back it up. Work experience offers a way to break the vicious cycle of 'no job equals no experience, but no experience equals no job'" she says.

Work experience can be invaluable if you have a vague idea about working to build communities but are not sure what's out there. A placement with the planning or housing department of your local authority can offer a useful insight, and provide helpful contacts.

Alternatively, there are some well-established programmes that are run by organisations including the thinktank Institute for Public Policy Research (the IPPR), RegenWM, which promotes regeneration in the heart of England, and Groundwork.

Groundwork, based in Oldham, offers a six-month, full-time work-experience programme for recent graduates of any discipline. Volunteers often go on to become one of Groundwork's 2,000 UK employees, or to work with one of the companies at which they did a placement during the course.

On the table: academic study or work experience?

Photo: courtesy of Hemingway Design

"My friends thought I was crazy when I decided to be a full-time volunteer with Groundwork," says Bianca Benini, who was disappointed to find herself working in retail despite achieving a Masters in Environmental Engineering. After the Groundwork course, she gained paid employment as marketing, sales and research officer for a recycling company in Manchester.

RegenWM arranges work experience placements in the regeneration sector in the West Midlands. Graduates join the scheme full time, while undergraduates can participate part time, alongside their studies. All placements offer expenses, and some even pay a salary. Of 20 graduates who have finished their placements since the scheme began two years ago, 17 are now employed full time in the sector.

Lauren Amery, 26, joined the RegenWM scheme after a degree in English, and was placed at consultancy Research House, where she is now employed.

"Despite witnessing the massive regeneration that Birmingham has been going through, I never really thought about jobs in regeneration," she says. "Now I've realised that I can build a career out of making a real difference to people's lives."

GRADUATE TRAINING

There are various graduate training schemes, which have the advantage of being paid and can also lead to a job on completion.

Government agency English Partnerships offers a two-year Graduate Development Programme, taking 12 graduates from any discipline who show a genuine interest in the sector.

Competition is fierce, with over 500 applicants last year. No surprise, since participants are paid £21,600 a year, with a projected salary of nearly £30,000 at the end. They work alongside a senior manager on a specific project, and also take placements in organisations including a Regional Development Agency.

Pamela Lewis, head of people development at English Partnerships, explains: "Our graduate programme is designed to ensure that you see the full breadth of regeneration across the whole country, without having to change jobs."

CAREER DEVELOPMENT

Once you have landed your first job, career development can be rapid. There's lots of professional training on offer. Among universities, more than 50 institutions offer postgraduate courses such as the Masters in Community Enterprise at the Judge Business School in Cambridge, or the Masters in Urban Regeneration at Sheffield Hallam.

"The course is vocational as well as academic, which means that it is genuinely as valuable as work experience," says Rachel Granger who teaches the Masters at Sheffield.

Once working in the sector, you can develop your skills and knowledge through the British Urban Regeneration Association's (BURA) UK-wide modular training programmes. Each programme consists of ten one-day courses on topics such as working with communities, economic development and achieving funding for projects. Participants can choose a few courses or take all ten, as part of a Postgraduate Certificate in Management. As well as gaining new skills, participants make contacts at all levels and from all over the country – and that's got to be good for job prospects.

"One of the main ways into regeneration is still through word of mouth and personal recommendation, so this networking is absolutely crucial," says Jess Steele, deputy chief executive at BURA.

DIRECT ROUTE

Careers in the regeneration and sustainable communities sectors are advertised weekly in the national press. Alternatively, you could go to one of the magazines specialising in the sector, such as New Start or Regeneration & Renewal. You can also register for relevant careers news at the Academy for Sustainable Communities website. ■

IPPR
www.ippr.org.uk

Groundwork
www.groundworkvpa.com

RegenWM
www.regenwm.org

English Partnerships
www.englishpartnerships.co.uk

BURA
www.bura.org.uk

Academy for Sustainable Communities
www.ascskills.org.uk

RESOURCES*

Give your sustainable communities career a head start with our selection of useful organisations and websites.

UMBRELLA BODIES

Action with Communities in Rural England
Aims to promote a healthy, vibrant and sustainable rural community sector that is well connected to policies and initiatives at national, regional, and local levels.
www.acre.org.uk

British Urban Regeneration Association
A key independent organisation in the field of regeneration, with a diverse cross-sectoral membership. Provides a forum for the exchange of ideas, experience and information in the sector, through events, training, research, awards and policy influence.
www.bura.org.uk

Economic Development Association Scotland
Aims to facilitate a substantial improvement in the effectiveness of economic development activity in Scotland through raising the knowledge, information and networks of those involved in all aspects of economic development.
www.edascot.org.uk

Local Government Association
Promotes the interests of English and Welsh local authorities – a total of just under 500 authorities, representing over 50 million people – and spends around £74 billion a year on local services.
www.lga.gov.uk

People for Action
National network of housing and regeneration organisations committed to sharing knowledge and practice to build strong communities.
www.pfanet.org.uk

Town and County Planning Association
An independent campaigning charity calling for more integrated planning based on the principles of accessibility, sustainability, diversity, and community cohesion.
www.tcpa.org.uk

REGIONAL DEVELOPMENT AGENCIES

RDAs are non-departmental public bodies set up by the government to promote sustainable economic development in England. Scotland, Wales and Northern Ireland also have their own Development Agencies.

Advantage West Midlands
www.advantagewm.co.uk

East of England Development Agency
www.eeda.org.uk

East Midlands Development Agency
www.emda.org.uk

London Development Agency
www.lda.gov.uk

Northwest RDA
www.nwda.co.uk

One Northeast
www.onenortheast.co.uk

South East England Development Agency
www.seeda.co.uk

South West of England Development Agency
www.southwestrda.org.uk

Yorkshire Forward
www.yorkshire-forward.com

Invest Northern Ireland
Main economic and development driver for Northern Ireland.
www.investni.com

Scottish Development Agency
The main economic development agency for Scotland.
www.scottish-enterprise.com

Welsh Development Agency
Stimulates and supports economic prosperity in Wales.
www.wda.co.uk

REGIONAL CENTRES OF EXCELLENCE

English regional bodies responsible for improving skills and knowledge in the fields of regeneration and sustainable communities.

Creating:excellence (for the Southwest)
www.creatingexcellence.org.uk

Future London
www.futurelondon.co.uk

Ignite (for the Northeast)
www.onenortheast.co.uk

Inspire East
www.inspire-east.org.uk

Regeneration East Midlands
www.regenerationem.co.uk

RegenWM (for the West Midlands)
www.regenwm.org

RENEW Northwest
www.renew.co.uk

Southeast Excellence
www.southeastexcellence.co.uk

Inclusion of an organisation or site does not necessarily imply endorsement by the publishers or partners of this guide.

MEDIA

New Start
A weekly magazine for all involved in community regeneration and social renewal. News, comment, analysis, jobs and public notices.
www.newstartmag.co.uk

Planning
The official journal of the Royal Town Planning Institute, a weekly serving everyone involved in planning and the built environment.
www.planning.haynet.com

Regeneration & Renewal
Sector weekly aimed at professionals involved in government-backed regeneration and community renewal projects.
www.regen.net

USEFUL ORGANISATIONS

Academy for Sustainable Communities
New national and international centre of excellence for the skills and knowledge needed to create local communities that are prosperous, lively and attractive to live in ASC works with partners to develop new learning resources, undertake major research studies, launch career drives and promote best practice.
www.ascskills.org.uk

Centre for Local Economic Strategies
An independent organisation involved in regeneration, local economic development and local governance. CLES brings together a network of subscribing organisations, including regeneration partnerships, local authorities, regional bodies and voluntary organisations.
www.cles.org.uk

Communities Scotland
A Scottish Executive agency that aims to work with others to ensure decent housing and strong communities across Scotland.
www.communitiesscotland.gov.uk

Community Development Foundation
A non-departmental public body helping communities achieve greater control over the conditions and decisions affecting their lives by advising government, supporting community work, and carrying out research, evaluation and policy analysis.
www.cdf.org.uk

Core Cities
Links the local authorities of the UK's major cities, to work together and share best practice in economic development and regeneration.
www.corecities.com

Development Trusts Association
Works towards a successful development trust in every community that wants one. There are over 300 development trusts across the UK, all community owned and led. They cultivate enterprise, build assets, and secure community prosperity.
www.dta.org.uk

Groundwork
A federation of trusts in England, Wales and Northern Ireland, each working with their partners to improve the quality of the local environment, the lives of local people and the success of local businesses in areas in need of investment and support.
www.groundwork.org.uk

Improvement and Development Agency
Government body that works with local councils on economic and community development, as well as improving services and consultation.
www.idea.gov.uk

Joseph Rowntree Foundation
One of the largest social policy research and development charities in the UK, spending about £7 million a year on programmes that seek to better understand the causes of social difficulties and explore ways of overcoming them.
www.jrf.org.uk

Neighbourhood Statistics
Provides free information and statistics on local issues such as employment, crime, work patterns and house prices.
neighbourhood.statistics.gov.uk

New Economics Foundation
An independent think-and-do tank aiming to improve quality of life by promoting innovative solutions challenging mainstream thinking on economic, environment and social issues.
www.neweconomics.org

Office of the Deputy Prime Minister
Government department responsible for regional economic development, regeneration and sustainable communities.
www.odpm.gov.uk

UK Communities Online
Aims to address issues of sustainability, regeneration, social inclusion and healthier economies by focusing on the use of new communications technologies in communities and neighbourhoods.
www.communities.org.uk

Urban Regeneration Companies
Promoted by the government and established by local partners, in order to achieve a focused, integrated regeneration strategy for key towns and cities. They produce a powerful and coherent single vision for the future of their entire area and then co-ordinate its implementation.
www.urcs-online.co.uk

ACADEMIC QUALIFICATIONS

University of Bradford
Foundation Degree in Active Citizenship and Participation
Designed for those involved in local government and voluntary organisations who are seeking to encourage more people to become active within their communities and to promote participation.

BA Community Regeneration and Development
A key feature of the course is its relationship to local and sub-regional developments in regeneration policy and practice. It has been designed in consultation with people engaged in community regeneration both in rural and urban areas.
www.bradford.ac.uk

Cardiff University
MSc Regeneration Studies
Allows students to examine the range of issues covered by regeneration studies, especially the interplay between economy, state and civil society. It will also furnish students with an opportunity to develop the analytical and social skills sought in today's regeneration-related professions.
www.cardiff.ac.uk

University of Central Lancashire
BSc Sustainable Design
The course provides students with up-to-date professional and academic training in sustainable design that is relevant to the needs of a career in sustainable development.
www.uclan.ac.uk

University of Derby
Foundation Degree in Community Regeneration and Development
This programme offers a multi-disciplinary approach and aims to increase the capacity and career opportunities of voluntary and paid workers in community regeneration and development.
www.derby.ac.uk

University of Glamorgan
Foundation Degree in Community Regeneration
This programme will give students a background in community regeneration issues. Students will identify future trends and acquire the confidence and skills essential to working in a community setting.

MSc Community Regeneration
Aims to provide community regeneration workers in the UK with a practical knowledge and theoretical understanding of contemporary community regeneration policy and practice.
www.glam.ac.uk

University of Gloucestershire
BA Rural Planning
Includes modules on local economies, consulting communities, the greening of local economies and the growth of science parks.

BA Community Development
Examines the principles and practice of developing communities in urban neighbourhoods, towns and rural areas, including study areas from community initiatives and changes in modern society.
www.glos.ac.uk

The University of Liverpool
BA Urban Regeneration and Planning
Provides an opportunity to gain a better understanding of how planning and associated activities can contribute to the regeneration of primarily urban areas.
www.liv.ac.uk

London South Bank University
Foundation Degree in Urban Regeneration and Community Development
Developed to meet the urgent needs of urban regeneration employers, practitioners and the large number of people who volunteer with urban regeneration agencies and organisations.
www.lsbu.ac.uk

Sheffield Hallam University
BA Urban Regeneration
The course covers the urban social sciences of geography, economics, sociology and politics. Study focuses on legal and planning constraints that affect urban development and change.

Masters in Planning
This degree is for people interested in improving and regenerating the environment in our towns, cities and countryside.
www.shu.ac.uk

University of the West of England, Bristol
BA Planning, Housing and Renewal
Subjects include urban design, making of place, planning policy and practice, sustainable development, the development process, social and economic analysis, the politics and philosophy of planning, and cities in transition. The course is accredited by the Chartered Institute of Housing.
www.uwe.ac.uk

NOTE: This is just a selection of the many regeneration and sustainable communities courses on offer. For a full list, try entering these as search terms at the UCAS website.
www.ucas.co.uk

ETHICAL
BUSINESS

IN THE RIGHT COMPANY

Few issues ignite debate about ethical careers more than corporate social responsibility. As **JOHN PLUMMER** asks: to change big business, is it better to work from the outside or within?

CORPORATE social responsibility (CSR) only entered the business lexicon a decade ago but already it is everywhere. Companies are falling over themselves to produce reports showing how seriously they take it; the government has a CSR minister and funds a CSR academy.

Even Coco de Mer's erotic emporium in London sells ethically sourced spanking paddles and leather handcuffs. No one, it seems, should have to suffer for capitalism unless they want to.

It means the boundaries for ethical careers have exploded far beyond their traditional voluntary sector hinterland. Today's conscientious career hunter can join a company's CSR team or a firm with sound ethical credentials instead of a charity and feel no less guilty.

At least that's the theory. Few topics provoke as much disagreement as CSR, which remains a somewhat nebulous concept. According to the government, it is "about how business takes account of its economic, social and environmental impacts in the way it operates." Some disagree and prefer to talk about 'sustainable development' or 'environmental reporting'; job titles can reflect this word play. Others claim the very idea of caring capitalism is an oxymoron.

Toby Wood, editor of Ethical Corporation magazine, agrees that

the CSR landscape is littered with mirages. He says one company hired a CSR person merely to get government approval for a takeover – and once that succeeded, the luckless recruit found their promised budget non-existent.

But, he adds, not all organisations are so insincere, and with practically every company in the FTSE 100 having some kind of environmental policy, CSR is fast emerging as a viable career choice.

Andrew Dunnett, director of the CSR Academy, agrees. "Judging by the number of emails we get, there is an increasingly number of people who want to make CSR a career option," he says.

Because CSR is still in its infancy there is no clear entry route, but academic courses are increasingly popular. "In the last five years there has been a significant growth in the number of business and management schools offering graduates training in different forms of CSR," says Dunnett, who predicts that university qualifications will soon be an essential entry-level requirement.

Institutions offering courses include Birkbeck College at the University of London, which runs an MSc in Corporate Governance and Business Ethics; Bath University School of Management, which offers an MSc in Responsibility and Business Practice, and Cambridge University, which runs an MA in CSR.

"Anybody who is serious about careers in CSR should consider these kinds of courses, but they should look closely at what they offer because they range from business ethics to social entrepreneurship," says Dunnett.

Potential recruits also require a sharp business brain. "Informed enthusiasm is great," says Andrew Shield, CSR manager at Thames Water. "But what's critical is a good appreciation of business realities.

"Nothing is going to endear you to an employer if you purely have the altruism that a good proportion of graduates come equipped with. It needs to come with an understanding that there are a whole lot of business drivers."

Shield gained experience as an engineer then worked with a non-governmental organisation in Uganda before getting into CSR. He leads a nine-strong team that operates independently of the press office. Some companies include CSR in their press team but that can suggest that ethics are little more than an extension of the corporate spin machine.

Shield's job is equally split between internal CSR issues, such as formulating environmental policies, and external issues, such as developing projects with partners such as the RSPB, WaterAid and Age Concern. Thames Water staff are entitled to two days extra leave each year to undertake charity work.

Charity partnerships are a major part of the job. As head of corporate responsibility at telecommunications company O2, Simon Davis oversees his company's three-year relationship with charity Weston Spirit, part of which involves organising 200 O2 staff to mentor young people at the charity.

"It's useful to acquire an interest in the charity sector," Davis advises recruits. A challenging aspect of CSR is assessing the impact of your work. "It's not easy to measure," he admits. "One measure is engagement: how many people are aware of the charity, how many of our staff are engaged in the mentoring programme."

Oil giant Shell, which employs 112,000 people worldwide, doesn't have a specific CSR team. "CSR is not limited to people in a separate function but is part of the way we do business," says a spokeswoman.

"In most cases we hire experienced people from business with a variety of educational backgrounds – not necessarily environmental but also technical. We look for people with good communication and engagement skills. We generally do not require specific degrees."

Joining a CSR team isn't the only way of showing you care. "You don't need to work in CSR to do CSR," says Lucy Shea, a partner in sustainability communications company Futerra. "You can do CSR in any business function and will probably be more effective than you would be producing fluffy brochures."

But locating a socially responsible employer isn't easy. Business in the Community runs an annual corporate responsibility index, listing the most responsible businesses and companies benchmarking against their peers. But it's a purely voluntary exercise judged more on intentions than outcomes.

Meanwhile, the online forum SEECompanies asks more rigorous questions, which is perhaps why fewer than 20 companies have answered them.

Toby Wood agrees that working in CSR isn't always the best way to go about saving the planet. "Most

CSR teams don't understand CSR," he says. "They end up working in 'CSR silos' preaching about issues they are isolated from. It's best to work elsewhere in the company first to get a picture of what the company does."

There are no easy ways to spot the difference between companies that care and charlatans that regard CSR as a way to 'greenwash' their bad practices. Even organisations as experienced in the field as WWF-UK, which has partnerships with no fewer than 18 businesses, admits as much. Its process of due diligence took two years before it agreed to work with HSBC.

"It all boils down to research," says Dax Lovegrove, business relations manager at WWF-UK. "You have to go through websites, annual reports and CSR reports. See if companies include numbers and metrics about their strengths and weaknesses – not many do." ▶

→**Corporate Watch**
www.corporatewatch.org

→**CSR Academy**
www.csracademy.org.uk

→**Government CSR website**
www.csr.gov.uk

→**Business in the Community**
www.bitc.org.uk

→**Friends of the Earth**
www.foe.co.uk

GO IT ALONE

Ever thought of setting up your own ethical business? **CASPAR VAN VARK** offers some tips.

IF YOU can't live without relaxing weekends, regular holidays and a reliable income, stop reading now. But if you like the idea of being your own boss and don't mind a bit of hardship, launching a business could be your ideal route to an ethical career.

So what is an ethical business? At one end of the scale there are ordinary companies with strong corporate social responsibility (CSR) policies – the kind of firm that organises annual fundraisers for a local charity, ploughs money into the community, then spends lots of cash telling you all about it. A company like the The Body Shop would be somewhere in the middle: ethics are at the heart of the brand, but it retains a conventional business model designed to make profits for shareholders. And then there are social enterprises: businesses that reinvest their surpluses to achieve social aims.

Starting up an ethical business is not vastly different from starting a regular business. In some ways, though, you are making life harder for yourself. Not only are you launching a business (always a tough job), but there's an added social and ethical dimension to build into the model. That said, ethical businesses are on the increase, and you can take advantage of dedicated support services to help you get off the ground.

FORMULATE YOUR IDEA

Like any business, you need to find a gap in the market. Ethical businesses are not charities, and if no one wants your product or service, you won't last. Gilly MacPherson launched urbanangel, an ethical café in Edinburgh, after travelling in Australia and New Zealand and noticing how well similar businesses were doing there. She sells only fair trade and ethically sourced products.

"I felt there was a niche here," she says. "I feel strongly about fair trade issues, but the opportunity for people to

drink fair trade coffee were limited, so I decided to make it easy for people to spend their money ethically by opening a stylish place where they will want to go."

Once you've got a basic idea for a business, how are you going to make sure it's ethical? It could just be the products you sell, such as Gilly's café. Alternatively, you can go further and work ethics into your financial model. Instead of putting all the profits in your pocket, you pay yourself a salary and reinvest the rest into social projects. And there are other ways of adding ethics to the equation too. Daily Bread, a food co-operative in Cambridge, employs people with mental health problems, paying them a fair wage and increasing their employability in other fields. The precise ethical makeup of your business really depends on you, and how far you want to take it.

DO YOUR HOMEWORK

It's impossible to do too much research. Gilly spent a year researching before she opened her café, and it's important to take on as much advice as possible.

"I went to the Business Gateway, used every service they had and went on every course," she says. "I'd definitely advise others to do the same."

Reed Paget, a former journalist, is co-founder of Belu, an ethically minded bottled water company. Belu's surpluses are used to fund clean water projects around the world. "I read a few books on setting up a company, and that was a good way

Photo: Urbanangel

"o start," he says. "And it's great to get advice from other entrepreneurs, if you can get their time. I also made sure I got people on my team with different skill backgrounds."

Use the internet, go to libraries, talk to people, go cn courses, and read books. All of this will give you a better chance of success.

GET FUNDING

This is often the trickiest part. If you're young with few assets and no financial track record, many banks will be reluctant to part with their cash. But

don't despair – there are lots of ways to get money. First of all, believe in your idea, and formulate a good business plan. The Government's Business Link service offers free advice and resources.

"Launching a business that has social objectives and not primarily profit ones makes it hard to get seed (early investment) capital," says Reed. "You might have an invention that cures cancer and saves the rainforest, but unless someone can get rich from it, it may never succeed. You'll

often have to put in a lot of elbow grease."

Try your own bank first, and be passionate about your business plan.

"Persuading banks to invest money comes down to your own commitment," says Peter Paduh, founder of Maxitech. His is an ethical business on several levels: it recycles used IT equipment and reinvests profits into social projects, as well as offering training to disadvantaged young people. It has an impressive business plan, but like most entrepreneurs, Peter had to work hard to persuade the bank to take a chance.

If high-street banks don't want to know, you can try more ethically minded lenders, such as Triodos Bank. Triodos is an ethical business itself, and funds others, including Gilly's urbanangel café.

"We view returns not just as profit, but as social returns," says Gareth Zahir-Bill, loan manager at Triodos. "We're interested in how people are affected by the business."

There are also grants and loans specifically aimed at young entrepreneurs, ethical or mainstream. Try the Prince's Trust, which offers market-testing grants of £250, and low-interest loans up to £5,000. UnLtd also funds young social entrepreneurs, and Social Enterprise Training and Support lists lots of funding sources on its website.

STICK TO YOUR IDEALS

You need the business to make money, but you also want to be true to your ideals. As an ethical business, you will appeal to people who share your values, but you may also be putting yourself at a disadvantage over your (less principled) competitors.

"I know how cheaply some of them come by their products," says Gilly. "So you have to be comfortable with the fact that you're not competing on the same level."

At the same time, you can't be so obsessed with your ideals that you fail to run a viable business. Donatella Versace's insistence that "more is more" may work for fashion, but when it comes to selling ethics, the reverse is true, says Belu's Reed Paget: "Don't market your ethics as your most important selling point," he advises. "People will get tired of it. First and foremost you need a high-quality product."

Setting yourself up as an ethical entrepreneur is never going to be easy – but is it worth it?

Absolutely. For Gilly, it means hard work and tight profit margins but the immeasurable satisfaction of doing something she truly believes in.

"I feel strongly about what I do," she says. "Yes, you're making it more difficult for yourself, but you just have to be clever and raise your game. This is more fulfilling than any other career I can think of." ◗

→ **Tridos Bank**
www.triodos.co.uk

→ **StartUps Website**
www.startups.co.uk

→ **Small Business Service**
www.sbs.gov.uk

→ **Business Link**
www.businesslink.gov.uk

→ **UnLtd**
www.unltd.org.uk

→ **National Council for Graduate Entrepreneurs**
www.ncge.org.uk

→ **The Princes Trust**
www.princes-trust.org.uk

→ **SETAS**
www.setas.co.uk

INVESTMENT MANAGER

Name: James Vaccaro
Age: 31

What makes your job so ethical? I'm an investment manager at Triodos, an ethical bank that only lends money to organisations that benefit people and the environment – projects like organic shops and wind farms.

What does your typical day involve? Often deals or negotiations need to be completed late at night so work doesn't take place in the day at all. My job revolves around negotiating renewable energy contracts between the various people involved in making a project happen, from technology suppliers and engineers to developers and large utility companies. At the same time I need to ensure that our renewable energy investment fund is running smoothly, and that the board and investors are informed about what we're doing.

Did you do any specific training or qualifications to get this job? Anyone working in investments needs to complete a Financial Services Authority-approved qualification. As with most jobs, the real training comes from the practical aspects.

How did you get into this job? After a year working for the student union, I came across Triodos, which was then quite a new ethical bank. I wrote to the managing director and was lucky enough to be offered a job.

What kind of personality is best suited to working in a job like yours? You certainly need tenacity. Because of their size, renewable energy deals are never straightforward. You've got to be confident that you can make it happen.

What skills and experience do you need to work in this sector? You need an understanding of the business world and finance, knowledge of contract law, and strong negotiation skills.

What's the most memorable experience you've had in this job? The opening of a wind project in north Wales. Three hill farmers were setting up a small wind farm on their land. Celebrating the project's opening on the side of a windy hill with the farmers, their families, and 1,000 local people was one experience I'll never forget.

Any top tips for someone wanting to get into this work? It's not easy and the competition will be fierce. Try and gain some work experience. Be ready and willing to put your all into the job. ❱

→**Triodos Bank**
t. 01179 739 339
e. mail@triodos.co.uk
www.triodos.co.uk

TRANSPORT PROJECT OFFICER

Name: Alexandra Allen
Age: 26

So, what do you actually do? I work with sustainable transport charity Sustrans to manage projects like Liveable Neighbourhoods, where we're working to redesign streets and other public space to make it easier, safer and nicer to walk and cycle.

What makes your job so ethical? I'm working towards a future in which people choose to travel in ways that benefit their health and the environment. Everything we do is focused on creating the right conditions for that, or providing information helping people to travel by bus, bike or on foot.

How did you get into this job? I started at Sustrans as a PA to the fundraising director, then worked as publications officer, before moving into project management.

What kind of personality is best suited to working in a job like yours? It's good to be flexible and enthusiastic. It definitely helps to be patient and good at communicating because the projects we deliver always involve many partners who range from being very supportive to downright unhelpful. It's usually up to us to keep everybody moving towards the final goal.

What skills and experience do you need to work in this sector? Not necessarily transport planning, that's for certain. I'm constantly amazed by the variety of roles that sit in my building: civil and traffic engineering, fundraising, geographic information systems technology, marketing and PR, I suspect the only thing we all have in common is a strong desire to see more people walking and cycling.

Best things about the job? Working in an organisation where the staff really care about what they do each day and seeing that you are making a difference.

And the most challenging? There's always more that could be done and sometimes it feels like there aren't enough days in the week to do it all. And, as a charity, we are always looking for funding for new projects, which can sometimes be quite stressful.

Any top tips for someone wanting to get into this work? I never wanted to be a PA but it was a way into the organisation. Once you're in, it's much easier to demonstrate that you could be doing more. ❱

➜Sustrans
t. 08451 130 065
e. info@sustrans.org.uk
www.sustrans.org.uk

WORK TO LIVE

Careers in social enterprise

A special supplement supported by:

Thinking about starting up your own business?
Want a free head start?

If you are thinking about starting up your own business and need a free head start then look no further than **www.businesslink.gov.uk**, the new Business Link website. Backed by Government, it's packed full of free tools to help you find the grants, funding and training you may need.

- Devise your business plan – follow our easy step-by-step process to create a plan to get your business off the ground.

- Raise finance successfully – use our guides to help you understand what types of finance are available, which ones are right for you and how to get further help and advice.

- There are a host of 'how to' guides covering everything from marketing to management.

- Take advantage of our easy to use tools – use our Licence and permit checklist and Regulation checklist to understand what you need to help you stay legal.

Give your new venture the
head start it deserves with
businesslink.gov.uk
Tel 0845 600 9 006

Business Link

"A social enterprise is a business with primarily social objectives whose surpluses are principally reinvested for that purpose in the business or in the community, rather than being driven by the need to maximise profit for shareholders and owners."

THE DEPARTMENT FOR TRADE AND INDUSTRY

INTRODUCTION

WELCOME to this careers supplement on the social enterprise sector.

If you have ever wondered whether there is a way to work in a business and give something back to society, then social enterprise could be the answer for you. If you want to use the skills you have acquired at school, college, university or in the workplace to create more than just a salary, then Work to Live is definitely for you. Over these pages we will explain exactly what people mean when they use the term 'social enterprise'. The guide illustrates the kind of opportunities that are out there for ethically motivated job seekers, and provides tips on how to land the perfect position in the career that was made for you.

Social Enterprise London is delighted to be involved with this guide. With the rise in popularity of ethical business, fair trade, co-operative working, not-for-profits and corporate social responsibility, the 21st century is alive with exciting ways of doing business. Read and enjoy this guide and make your way to the front of this exciting new movement.

Don't forget to contact us with your own success story. Good luck!

ALLISON OGDEN-NEWTON
Chief executive

social **enterprise** london

www.sel.org.uk

THE BIG PICTURE

What are social enterprises? As PAUL ALLEN reports, they're all around you.

TONY BLAIR has called them "radical new ways to boost our economy". TV chef Jamie Oliver is arguably their most famous proponent in Britain. But what exactly are social enterprises?

If you have ever bought a cup of fair trade coffee, or a copy of The Big Issue, you're already one step closer to the answer. Social enterprises are like any other company. They exist to make profit. But, it's what they do with the money, and how they make it, that makes them special.

Instead of handing over the spoils to management boards and faceless shareholders, social enterprises reinvest their profits into good causes. For many, the very operation of the business has social outcomes: the employment of people with learning difficulties for example, or creating a fairer market for chocolate producers in the developing world.

It's a simple concept, combining the best bits of the charity and private sectors. But why not just be a charity? Unlike voluntary organisations, most social enterprises are financially self-sufficient, which means they don't have to rely on handouts. Charities can be left high and dry when grant money runs out, leaving projects frustratingly incomplete, while extra funding frequently comes with strings attached.

Social enterprises are free of these complications. By building successful companies in their own right, profits can be spent on social aims. There's a staggering diversity among social businesses, but each one shares a common goal: to give something back.

In recent years, the government has begun to recognise the power of the sector. One advantage of social enterprises is that they often have a good understanding of the needs of local people. Because they pursue two goals – profit and social wellbeing (known as the 'double bottom line') – they are ideally placed to deliver local community services.

What's more, the challenge of making money ethically often produces some truly innovative ideas. Just take a look at these famous success stories.

THE BIG ISSUE

"We're a hand up, not a hand-out," says Patrick Lisoire at The Big Issue. "The whole point of the magazine is to give homeless people an alternative to begging."

Established 14 years ago in London, The Big Issue today prints five regional editions and sells 155,000 copies a week. The concept is simple: homeless people buy the magazine for 60p, resell it to the public for £1.40, and keep the difference.

"With a product to sell, our vendors become small businesspeople," explains Patrick. "That really helps to boost their self-esteem, motivation and sense of worth."

Besides selling to vendors, the magazine also makes money through advertising. As a social enterprise, any profits go to good causes – in this case, The Big Issue Foundation, a registered charity. The foundation helps homeless people find jobs, training and education, and provides advice on health, housing and finance.

"The Big Issue is a great social tool," says Patrick. "Not only do we produce a magazine that rivals the big newspapers, we're also allowing thousands of homeless people to move on with their lives."

FIFTEEN

Before Jamie Oliver got stuck into school dinners, the TV chef had already established his social credentials with the 2002 show Jamie's Kitchen. The idea – to transform a group of disadvantaged youngsters into top class chefs – proved a huge hit.

The TV cameras may have stopped rolling, but the training programme keeps on going. To date, 37 trainees have 'graduated' from the east London restaurant Fifteen.

"Fifteen has been about taking raw enthusiasm and shaping it into something incredibly rewarding," says Jamie. "I know for a fact there are some in the Fifteen brigade who will go on to make some serious splashes in the restaurant world."

All profits from the restaurant go to the Fifteen Foundation, the charity that manages the annual training programme. The foundation has also turned the restaurant into a global model for social enterprise – there is already a Fifteen in Amsterdam, and Fifteen Melbourne is set to open in summer 2006.

CAFÉDIRECT

Cafédirect is a truly trailblazing social enterprise. The very first fair trade coffee company in the UK, it was founded in 1991 to help producers in South and Central America survive plummeting coffee prices. Since then, fair trade has become a hugely successful movement. During 2004, UK sales of fair trade goods rose by 51 percent to a retail value of over £140 million.

The fair trade movement is rooted in paying growers a decent, living wage. Last year, Cafédirect paid more than £2.4 million above market prices to coffee producers, and invested eight percent of gross profits back into business development programmes. Thanks to these, local growers and their families are starting to look to the future with renewed confidence.

"The balance between financial and social return is at the heart of our work," says Helen Ireland at Cafédirect. "It means we often have to be very innovative, and that makes it a really exciting place to work."

ECT GROUP

ECT Group, originally Ealing Community Transport, is one of the most diverse social enterprises in the country. What started out as a local voluntary organisation in west London has become a national market leader in recycling, engineering and community transport services.

"What makes ECT a social enterprise is our commitment to delivering positive social and environmental impacts, as well as being economically viable," says managing director Andy Bond.

"We are run on a not-for-profit basis – revenues are invested back into the business helping us continually improve what we do, making a difference to individuals, communities and the environment."

It's a winning strategy. In 2005, ECT recorded a turnover of £29 million. The group currently employs 900 staff.

"Our employees have a high degree of autonomy," says Andy. "It makes ECT a great place to work because people can realise their full potential." ∎

TIM SMIT
Chief executive
The Eden Project
www.edenproject.com

"If you have a great idea that can effect social change, spend time asking what factors need to be in place to make it successful and then ruthlessly find the people that compensate for your lack of skills."

GLL – The UK's Largest Leisure Trust

www.gll.org

As 'The Social Enterprise of the Year' National Award winner 2004, GLL continues to develop a national reputation for the provision of quality leisure services to all sectors of the community through a genuine Trust Management route. A founding member of SPORTA (the associated body for leisure trusts), GLL is committed to ensuring that the Trust route in leisure management is the best route for customers and staff.

GLL operates 48+ leisure centres across London and works in partnership with many local authorities and partners to provide a 'five star' leisure service at a '3 star' price to all members of the community. GLL is the largest leisure centre operator in London.

As a worker owned and controlled organisation, we offer career opportunities and benefits that far exceed the rest including:

- A desire to develop long term working relationships and 'home grow' the managers of the future
- Salaries that pay in the upper quartile of the Industry
- Top pension schemes
- A training culture which encourages continuous learning through training academies
- Nationally recognised external training courses such as our award winning Graduate Trainee Management Scheme and Lifeguard Training & Employment Academy
- Provision of training opportunities through the London Leisure College
- Opportunities to become a director in a £ multi million organisation and have a say in how the company is run

GLL is growing and needs loyal, enthusiastic and dynamic people with a 'can do' attitude, to develop the business with us. GLL offer a range of positions from:

Lifeguards and Sales and Fitness Staff to Duty Managers and General Managers.

SOUND LIKE YOU ?

To obtain an information pack and application form, contact dulce.benedicto@gll.org, or look up our website at www.gll.org.

We are an equal opportunities employer and applications are encouraged from all sections of the community. GLL is a non-smoking organisation.

GLL working in partnership with the London Boroughs of Barnet, Camden, Epsom & Ewell Borough Council, Greenwich, Hackney, Hammersmith & Fulham, Merton, Newham, Tower Hamlets, Waltham Forest, Bellingham Community Project & Sport England and the London Development Agency.

INVESTOR IN PEOPLE

Awarded for excellence

BRIGHT HORIZONS

Everyone has heard of business wonderkids who make their first million before they reach 25. Well, the social enterprise sector depends on its own bright young things.

Meet three inspiring young entrepreneurs pursuing social enterprise in very different ways.

HEATHER WILKINSON, 26

"It's so exhilarating, committing to the idea of setting up a social enterprise full time. From that moment on, you realise everything is going to change, the future is in your own hands, and only you can make it work."

Heather Wilkinson (above, left) is a networker. There's little she likes more than meeting new people, sharing new ideas and getting excited about the

potential that working on new and innovative projects can bring. She first learned about social enterprise doing a Geography degree at Southampton, and then completed a Masters in Community Enterprise at Birmingham University.

Her academic research into what social enterprise can achieve, as well as a strong social concience, led to her combining the two in Striding Out. It's a social enterprise that brings together and supports young people, aged 18-30, who want to set up their own enterprises.

"I finally felt it was time to take the plunge, and set up one of my own," she says. "I decided I would create my perfect job by combining all the aspects of work I enjoy – young entrepreneurship, social enterprise and corporate social responsibility."

Through Striding Out, young people with business ideas can meet together, share experiences, learn from each other and, who knows, even go into a business partnership together. Profit from the company is re-invested back into furthering its aims.

"We are keen to celebrate enterprise, and promote good work that is being undertaken, ultimately to inspire others," says Heather. "I love meeting inspirational people on a daily basis, and having the freedom to pursue innovative ideas and aspirations."

JASON PEGLER, 30

When Jason Pegler (opposite page, middle) set up Chipmunkapublishing, in 2002, it was not from a desire to be a business leader but to voice some of his own very personal experiences, and to offer others the opportunity to do the same.

"From the moment I realised I had a mental illness, I had a mission and a dream," says Jason. "My mission was to one day tell the whole world about the humiliation and guilt I had for having all those idiotic manic thoughts."

The first step to fulfilling his dream was to publish a book about his own experiences, A Can of Madness. Jason realised his work had not only helped him come to terms with his illness, it had begun to break down taboos about mental illness in wider society. So Jason used the proceeds of the 300 copies of the book he had printed to set up Chipmunka,

a social enterprise that specialises in publishing that enables people with mental illness to tell their stories and challenge the status quo.

"I set up the company to give a voice to the mentally ill," says Jason. "The role of Chipmunka is to change the way people think about mental health and to treat it as normal."

The publisher's books are written by people with mental health problems. By the end of 2005 it will have published 20 paperbacks and 100 e-books. The aim is to expand the business to publishing by, and for, other vulnerable sections of society.

"Chipmunkapublishing empowers its authors and encourages them to become self-publicists," says Jason, who in 2005 won the Young Entrepreneur of the Year Award. "Once published, authors become pro-active mouthpieces for the mental health movement."

TARA MCCONAGHY, 33

When Tara McConaghy (page 106, right) was at school, she did voluntary work with her mother, working in soup kitchens for homeless people. But after university she drifted into the corporate sector, working in finance.

"It was so boring," says Tara. "I felt empty and I wondered: 'Is this all that life involves?'"

Six years later, a serious illness prompted Tara to reconsider. She started working with a different kind of financial institution: one whose sole aim was to raise money for projects to improve children's education.

"All of a sudden I saw there were all these really exciting, sophisticated, professional people who were applying their skills, knowledge, and resources to furthering a social cause," she says.

Inspired, she set up her own social enterprise called LA Edupreneurs, which links up head teachers, schools and educationalists with business people and others who want to help improve education.

"It brought people together. I got millionaires actually talking to teachers working in very deprived areas," she says.

Tara decided to take her interest in social enterprise one step further: she enrolled in the Masters programme at Skoll Centre for Entrepreneurship, the Oxford-based business school specialising in social enterprise. As part of the programme, she helped Jamie Oliver develop plans to expand his 'Fifteen' social enterprise and worked at Participant Productions, a Hollywood film company set up to produce blockbuster films with a strong social message.

"If you are inspired to dedicate your professional career to serving others, there are career paths for you," she says. "So just charge ahead!" ■

Striding Out
www.stridingout.co.uk

Skoll Centre for Social Entrepeneurship
www.sbs.ox.ac.uk/html/faculty_skoll_main.asp

Chipmunkapublishing
www.chipmunkapublishing.com

"To successfully work in the sector, values are more important than qualifications, drive more important than background and commitment to social change more important than anything."

TOP TIP

DAI POWELL
Chief executive
Hackney Community Transport
www.hackneyct.org

Name Rachel
Sharpley

Age 28

FAIR TRADE MARKETING ASSISTANT

So, what do you actually do? A wide range of things, from delivering educational talks to meeting confectionery buyers, working on marketing and sampling campaigns. One of my favourite roles is taking our new chocolate fountain to events.

What makes Divine a social enterprise? Divine chocolate was set up to improve the lives of cocoa farmers in Ghana through selling fair trade chocolate in the UK. The co-operative of farmers that grow the cocoa for Divine owns a third of the company and have seats on the board. So they really do have a say, from bean to bar.

Did you need any specific education or training to get into this job? I studied International Relations and Geography at St Andrews University. I think my background in development studies and work on development projects helped.

How did you get into this job? I'd been thinking about what a great idea fair trade was for a while. When I saw an entrance-level job advertised in the paper for a job working in a fair trade chocolate company, I decided to take the plunge.

What does your typical day involve? There is no typical day. Last night I did a talk at a workshop to encourage London councils to switch to fair trade. This morning I packed 80 Divine hampers to promote our chocolate in stores across the UK. I also spoke to a journalist who had agreed to run a piece in the paper in return for some chocolate for a children's charity fundraiser. I worked with colleagues on our website, I spoke to customers about prices and marketing materials, and arranged meetings with other organisations that promote fair trade. The only thing every day has in common is that I eat lots of chocolate!

What kind of personality is best suited to working in a job like yours? You have to enjoy talking to people, be creative, flexible, good at juggling a variety of tasks and be able to prioritise. You need to be passionate about fair trade, with the business skills and know-how to actually progress it.

What's the most memorable experience you've had in this job? Accompanying Ghanaian cocoa farmers on their fair trade fortnight tour of Britain, hearing how fair trade makes a difference to them and seeing the public understand that they can make a difference.

Divine Chocolate
t. 020 7378 6550
e. info@divinechocolate.com
www.divinechocolate.com

Divine chocolate: business ethos empowering farmers in the developing world

A STEP IN THE RIGHT DIRECTION

A background in the world of private business is the ideal springboard into social enterprise. ROSE SMITH talks to those who have made the change.

'I'D HAD enough of chasing the pound," says John Montague of his decision to leave the private sector after a 17-year career in construction. "We didn't train anyone because all the work was outsourced and we didn't engage with the communities we worked in. I felt I could be getting more out of the process."

A desire to lead a more fulfilling career is one reason why many in the private sector decide to move

across, into social enterprise. Montague, who is now chief executive of NewLife, a building company that trains unemployed young people, finds his greatest satisfaction is in creating opportunity. Helping to build people's lives, as well as their homes, can achieve tangible results. One of NewLife's trainees has just received an award from the Young Builders Trust.

"She was excluded from school at 15 and told she

wouldn't amount to much," says Montague. "Now she has an NVQ 2 and a trade. That makes me feel better than any amount of profit could do."

Wanting to make a career change is another common reason for moving between sectors. Sinead McBrearty felt she'd drifted into her marketing position at an accountancy firm and although she was successful, she wanted to find a more satisfying job.

"I had no clue what I wanted to do. So I went travelling for a year, to create space between one career and the next," she says. On her return she got a job as director of business services at Social Enterprise London, the agency tasked with promoting the sector in the capital. "My job is so much more interesting now. Social entrepreneurs have such passion and ambition – it's a very stimulating environment to work in."

The search for a different, more rewarding career provides the impetus to move across, but how easy is it to use your private-sector skills and experience in the social economy? It depends on the role, says Shaun Doran, commercial director of the Furniture Resource Centre, a furnishing and removals social enterprise in Liverpool.

"We recruit people from the private sector for specific areas. For a business development position, for example, commercial experience is invaluable as that person understands the realities of running a business. However, these skills wouldn't be top of the list for someone in our People and Learning Department," he says.

The Day Chocolate Company exists to improve the lives of farmers in West Africa, not through development work, but by selling bars of fair trade chocolate. Managing director Sophi Tranchell says: "We are meeting our objectives by building the Divine brand in the UK. My commercial skills gained in the private sector have therefore been very useful in working to achieve this."

Even a few years spent in the private sector can be of benefit to social enterprises, according to Adrian Clarke, business development manager of Green-Works, a company that recycles office furniture.

"If you get a graduate marketing job for a large private-sector brand where you can learn a lot, you can then take that experience across with you," he says.

A key step in moving across is to find out how to apply your skills from the private sector to the world of social enterprise, says Adrian. He spent nine years as a litigation solicitor before changing sectors.

"I didn't believe the skills I had to offer from the private sector would have been much use to a small, grant-funded charity so I applied for a job at Green-Works,

NewLife training: practical and life skills

which was a start-up with a strong commercial edge."

After you've researched the different kinds of organisations you'd like to work for, try to network with people working within them and if necessary pick up the phone and start cold-calling.

"And if an opportunity comes up, take it," says Sinead McBrearty at Social Enterprise London. "Moving across from a private-sector company into a social enterprise can feel scary, like you're stepping off the edge of something familiar, but it's definitely worth it."

Leaving behind the structured working environment of the private sector is one part of the transition process into social enterprise. There's often not too much money sloshing around, so there isn't such a network of support staff, which you can become used to in the private sector. It's more a case of mucking in, doing things yourself that you may have had an assistant for in the past.

Learning to think differently was part of the transition for Shaun Doran at the Furniture Resource Centre, when he moved from a career in the timber industry. "In the private sector, even though there's

talk of corporate social responsibility, things are more one-dimensional and move at a certain pace. However, in a social enterprise, everything has to be thought through because of the need to fulfil social goals. The speed is slower but you learn to tailor your expectations to suit the reality of a different environment."

One other major difference between sectors is salary, which in the social sector tends to be lower. However, Sophi Tranchell believes that job satisfaction and flexible working practices more than compensate. "Everyone at the Day Chocolate Company is so motivated because Divine chocolate is a fantastic idea," she says. "We're showing you can do business in a better way and still do well, and that gives everyone a kick."

Earning less to gain more in terms of job and personal satisfaction is a neat summary of the rationale behind a move from the private sector into the social economy. And with the number of social enterprises continuing to grow, if you've had enough of chasing the pound and want to put your skills to better use, now could be a good time to make the change. ∎

NewLife
www.newlife-build.co.uk

Social Enterprise London
www.sel.org.uk

Furniture Resource Centre
www.frcgroup.co.uk

"Don't think you have to choose between the cut and thrust of business and the warm glow of working for a charity or in the public sector, because social enterprise really does offer the best of both worlds."

JONATHAN BLAND TOP TIP
Chief executive
Social Enterprise Coalition
www.socialenterprise.org.uk

Name Lucy Hoyle
Age 25

GREEN ENERGY PROJECT DEVELOPER

So, what do you actually do? I'm project developer for Ecotricity, a green energy supplier. I prepare environmental impact assessments and planning applications for wind energy developments, including pre-application consultation and negotiations.

How is your company a social enterprise? Ecotricity is an ethically-minded company. We see ourselves as environmentalists doing business, and not the other way round. When Ecotricity started out it was the world's first renewable energy company.

Did you do any specific education or training that helped you get this job? I went to Oxford Brookes University to study Environmental Policy and Planning, and I did a Masters which led onto a further two years to gain a PhD.

How did you get into this job? Through my studies I became interested in renewable energy and, specifically, wind turbines. I applied to Ecotricity as they both build turbines and supply green electricity.

What does your typical day involve? Managing the site consultation process to identify which sites require further assessment studies, preparing environmental statements involving technical writing and research, and the day-to-day management of individual planning applications. Also, setting out the planning case for wind turbine developments and providing professional advice on site selection.

What skills and experience do you need to work in this sector? Some relevant experience of working with planning authorities is certainly useful, as is a background in the built environment, renewable technology or something similar.

What are the best things about your job? It doesn't get better than winning a planning application. After you've put months of hard work in, it's really satisfying to see a project get off the ground.

Any top tips for someone wanting to get into this work? Be prepared to get knocked down sometimes, but remain determined and, most importantly, be green at heart.

Ecotricity
t. 01453 756 111
e. info@ecotricity.co.uk
www.ecotricity.co.uk

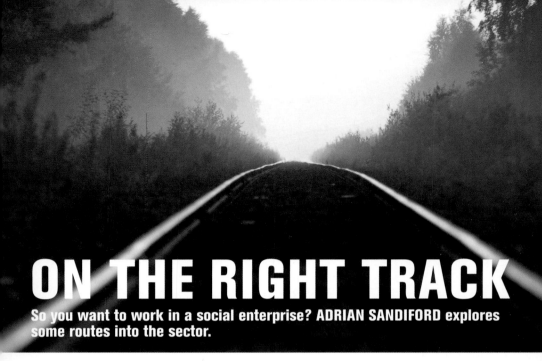

ON THE RIGHT TRACK

So you want to work in a social enterprise? ADRIAN SANDIFORD explores some routes into the sector.

IF THIS special social enterprise supplement has done its job, you should be dead keen to get involved. But what makes you think the social enterprises out there want you as an employee?

"The key to social enterprises is the values they're based on, so social enterprise employers need people who share those same values," says Ian Baker, development executive at the School for Social Entrepreneurs, an education programme dedicated to releasing entrepreneurial talent.

But sound environmental and ethical values aren't enough. The business side of social enterprise is just as important: after all, that's the way their social objectives are achieved. To be a good social enterprise employee, generous doses of business savvy and dynamism are vital ingredients in the mix.

You don't have to have run a business empire from your folks' garage, but you do need to show you've done something relevant and constructive with your time.

"We want to look at what other projects candidates have been involved in," says Adam Chetter, development manager at talentSTAR, an arts social enterprise that aims to help communities establish their own media projects. "It's not about just going for a job interview – you've got to try and build up a portfolio for the future."

THE DIRECT ROUTE

Like applying for a job in any organisation, the most obvious route is to take the traditional approach: job advert, interview, bingo! Think about the particular sector of social enterprise you want to work in. Don't take a scatter-gun approach, but hone your applications towards the particular field that most interests you.

Large social enterprises advertise in sector publications like Social Enterprise magazine, The Guardian 'Society' section, and The Times 'Public

Agenda' section, but it's worth keeping an eye on local papers too.

Organisations working in specialist fields will often bypass the national media, only advertising in relevant industry titles. Disability Now or Recycling Weekly, anyone? It's also worth networking and meeting organisations – personal contacts can help a lot.

Finally, do your homework. Use the potential employers' website to find out what the organisation is about.

"It's surprising that lots of people don't even bother to do basic research," says Andy Bindon at Greenwich Leisure, one of the UK's largest social enterprises.

WORK EXPERIENCE

There's a lot to be said for enthusiasm, but experience talks. A perfect way to get a foot in the door is to find work experience with similar organisations. The recycling and environment company Green-Works is one social enterprise that takes on interns, recruiting at careers fairs, through word of mouth and occasionally advertising via universities.

One recent intern, Charmaine Brown, a second-year student from Leeds University, was asked to collate an environmental sustainability report for the organisation. For the work she did, she won the 2005 Shell Technology Enterprise Programme Award.

GRADUATE TRAINING

Some of the larger social enterprises, particularly housing associations and leisure businesses, have graduate trainee schemes.

Greenwich Leisure was one of the first social enterprises to run a graduate training scheme. GLL has been crowned London's best employer for practical learning among 14-to-25-year-olds, and was finalist in the National Training Awards. Its award-winning graduate scheme now takes on ten trainee managers a year.

"It's a two-year scheme where graduates will get good experience in all areas of the business, and they also get to train for relevant qualifications in the leisure industry" says Andy Bindon, director of human resources.

Graduate training is a great way to make your mark. Over 70 percent of GLL's former trainees are still with the company, most in senior positions.

"Trainees can expect to go into an assistant manager position on finishing, and even become centre manager between 12 and 18 months later," says Andy. "We're looking for people who have a keen interest in the leisure industry but want to combine that with a social agenda. To understand our ethos that to achieve our agenda, we need to be a successful business. Business is a powerful catalyst for social change."

Trainees are expected to demonstrate what GLL calls its ten 'GeLL Factors', including a can-do attitude, a commitment to social aims and experience of working in a team.

THE ACADEMIC APPROACH

In universities, there are social enterprise-specific qualifications on offer, and there are other private sector courses and training available too.

The Judge Business School at Cambridge University offers a Masters in Community Enterprise, in association with the Development Trusts Association. The University of Leicester offers a Certificate of Higher Education in Social

Enterprise. The University of East London offers a BA in Social Enterprises, while Nottingham University offers a Social Enterprise module as part of its Masters in Entrepreneurship. The School for Social Entrepreneurs has a range of academic and hands-on programmes. (See the resources directory on page 122.)

Chris Mahon at the Institute for Enterprise and Innovation at Nottingham University Business School explains that where these courses will get you depends on your own goals and motivations.

"Courses that provide this type of training can help social entrepreneurs build enterprises that support and sustain their social missions, by leveraging business skills and strategies traditionally associated with the private sector," he says.

BE A SELF STARTER

If you've got a great idea and the entrepreneurial spirit, why not start your own social enterprise? Funding, advice and help is available.

UnLtd is a charity that provides grants and support to social entrepreneurs to start up and run projects that deliver social benefit.

Awards for individuals with new ideas can range between £500 and £5,000.

A number of networks also offer support and information, from Social Enterprise London to the Community Action Network, or the Small Business Service.

Striding Out is a social enterprise set up by 26-year-old Heather Wilkinson, to support young people with enterprising ambitions aged between 18 and 30.

Heather says setting up any business is a challenge, but one that provides a great learning opportunity for a young entrepreneur like her.

"It is important to find the perfect social enterprise idea that will enable you to combine work with pleasure," she advises. "Setting up and running a business is time and resource intensive, so it has to be a venture that you enjoy and want to spend time on, even at weekends."

As a self-starter with the right vision, you can have ownership of your project, achieve your ambitions, and achieve real social change. Research what's out there, and be imaginative: you're an entrepreneur. ∎

Green Works
www.green-works.co.uk

Greenwich Leisure
www.gll.org

talentSTAR
www.talentstar.net

School for Social Entrepreneurs
www.sse.org.uk

"Make sure you understand what it means to be a social enterprise and the ethics behind it. A practical, common sense, can-do attitude can be more important than a relevant degree."

TOP TIP

ANDY BOND
Managing director
ECT Group
www.ectgroup.co.uk

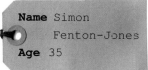

Name Simon Fenton-Jones

Age 35

CHIEF EXECUTIVE

So, what do you actually do? I run a professional shoe-shine business in city offices that trains, employs and supports people who have been homeless.

What makes the company a social enterprise? The 'shiners' are referred to StreetShine by participating homeless organisations. They receive training, a regular income and a bank account. The work gives them a route back into mainstream employment and allows them to develop their own franchise business, as well as improving their confidence, skills and self esteem.

How did you get into this job? I spent several years managing a pig-breeding business in a remote part of Vietnam. Probably not the most straightforward of routes, but it gave me incredible management experience, resilience and the ability to cope with any situation. On return, I couldn't face a 'normal' job, so I helped to set up a homeless football charity. After gaining management experience in the private and voluntary sectors, I was ideally placed to combine both in social enterprise.

What does your typical day involve? Meeting potential customers at a city firm in the morning followed by recruiting at a homeless hostel in the afternoon. In between, I'll be meeting current employees and helping them maximise their business, as well as sorting out employment issues such as benefits and bank accounts.

What kind of personality is best suited to working in a job like yours? You need an ability to get on with people, a problem-solving approach, to be open minded, up for a challenge and fairly relaxed, while maintaining a professional service for customers.

What skills and experience do you need to work in this sector? Without a good business plan and sound business skills, you cannot achieve your social aims.

What's the most memorable experience you've had in this job? Seeing an employee use his first pay cheque to move from sleeping rough under a bridge into a flat. I'm motivated by inspiring people to maximise their potential.

Any top tips for someone wanting to get into this work? Get as much experience as you can and start applying, as well as networking in the social enterprise sector.

StreetShine
t. 020 7840 3468
e. simon@streetshine.com
www.streetshine.com

SE=DA

**SOUTH EAST
ENGLAND
DEVELOPMENT
AGENCY**

Working for England's World Class Region

SEEDA is the Government funded agency responsible for the economic and social development of the South East of England.

THE SOUTH EAST really is a driving force of the UK's economic life. As home to over eight million people, covering the counties of Berkshire, Buckinghamshire, Hampshire, the Isle of Wight, Kent, Oxfordshire, Surrey and East and West Sussex, the South East is bigger than

Scotland, Wales and Northern Ireland combined.

THE REGION'S economy is the 22nd largest in the world, bigger than several countries including Denmark, Austria, Sweden, South Africa, Singapore and Greece.

SEEDA aims is to create a prosperous, dynamic and inspirational region by helping businesses compete more effectively, training a highly skilled workforce, supporting and enabling our communities,

while safeguarding our natural resources and cherishing our rich cultural heritage.

WE ARE a catalyst for change, working in the South East with partner organisations, businesses, schools and colleges, local authorities, Government agencies, voluntary and community groups, and many others.

THE CHALLENGES we face come in many forms: social exclusion, housing and skills shortages,

WORKING WITH SOCIAL ENTREPRENEURS

Social Entrepreneurship has a vast role to play in the South East.

In 2005 The South East Social Enterprise Steering group launched its regional framework for social enterprise. This framework seeks to develop the infrastructure to support the development of social enterprise, within the context of the wider economy.

Working in partnership with 16 agencies, we are working to develop new markets where social entrepreneurs can operate, from environmental business, to ethical trade, culture, regeneration and housing.

We have created a network of county development partnerships throughout the region and will be working closely with them to support the integration of social enterprise and entrepreneurship into local public, private and voluntary and community sector organisations.

This is a new and exciting time for social entrepreneurs in the South East and we are doing all we can to give opportunities for exploration and innovation.

environmental damage and over stretched public services.

THE CONTINUED success of our region depends on the realisation that business, environmental and social goals are all inextricably linked. Sustainable communities depend on sustainable business and vice versa.

AS WE move into the 21st century, it is becoming increasingly clear that our productivity and therefore our competitiveness depends on the ability of our region to release more people into economic activity.

WE NEED to meet demands for new skills, invest in efficient infrastructure and housing and address the economic and social consequences of globalisation and demographic change at the local level.

SEEDA is committed to developing the people and the skills the South East needs to meet these challenges.

FIND OUT MORE ABOUT **SEEDA**, AND THE WORK WE'RE DOING TO SUPPORT SOCIAL ENTERPRISE.

TEL. 01483 484200
EMAIL. SarahLinington@seeda.co.uk
www.seeda.co.uk

Name Daniel Drummond

Age 29

COMMUNITY DEVELOPMENT WORKER

So, what do you actually do? I am a development worker at the Black Health Agency in Manchester, which promotes health equality for black and minority ethnic (BME) communities, through a range of local regional and national services. It's been recognised that there is a low number of drug users from BME communities accessing treatment, so part of my role is bridging the gaps between drug service delivery and BME drug users' needs, by setting up projects, developing partnerships and informing local strategies.

How is your company a social enterprise? We are a voluntary sector charity and company limited by guarantee, and although most of services do not produce surpluses, we do generate funds through training on diversity, which I help deliver.

Did you do any specific education or training that helped you get this job? I've got a diploma in Social Science and a degree in Sociology. Although having an academic background is important, I think it was more about my experience. I've worked in both the voluntary and private sectors. It's not always about the jobs you've done but more about recognising the skills you've gained.

What does your typical day involve? It can be anything from writing reports, delivering training, doing presentations, visiting community groups or services and, most importantly, developing solutions to race equality issues.

What kind of personality is best suited to working in a job like yours? Anyone that has a strong ability to connect with communities. You also need to learn from your mistakes and learn from those around you.

What's the most memorable experience you've had in this job? Taking young people who had been excluded from school on a residential event to London looking at drug issues in their local areas.

What are the best things about your job? I enjoy nearly everything about it. It's nice working on different levels, from grassroots work with communities to strategic planning and project development.

What are your top tips for someone wanting to get into this work? Take every opportunity that comes your way, and recognise all your experiences as valuable, whether they are good or bad!

Black Health Agency
t. 01618 752 052
e. info@blackhealthagency.org.uk
www.blackhealthagency.org.uk

1.2%
Percentage of UK businesses that are social enterprises

1 in 5
Proportion of social enterprises that earn more than £1 million a year

1 in 50
Proportion of UK workforce employed by social enterprises

25%
Average income social enterprises earn from selling goods or services

£18bn
Total turnover of the UK social enterpr se sector, each year

10
Number of people employed by a typical social enterprise

80
Number of local leisure services that are social enterprises

1 in 5
Proportion of social enterprises locatec in London

15,000
Number of social enterprises in the UK

Source: Small Business Service, July 2005

RESOURCES

In association with

UNLTD supports people who have the ideas and the commitment to make a difference in their communities. It provides a package of funding and support, to help these individuals establish projects that deliver social benefit.

LEVEL 1 Awards of between £500 and £5,000 are for individuals with new ideas, who want the opportunity to put them into practice.

LEVEL 2 Awards can be up to £20,000 and are for exceptional individuals who are applying innovative solutions to social problems.

www.unltd.org.uk

FINANCE

Community Development Finance Association
Trade association of community development finance institutions, providing financial investment in disadvantaged communities.
www.cdfa.org.uk

Charities Aid Foundation
CAF provides specialist financial services to charities and their supporters. It provides grants for any charitable organisation, with some funds specifically targeted at organisations with an annual income of up to £50,000.
www.cafonline.org

Access Funds
Access Funds aims to provide the latest funding information from central government, National Lottery, devolved governing bodies, the EU and quangos. The site has a wide range of services to help you fundraise and also contains directories of funding programmes and guides to funding.
www.access-funds.co.uk

London Rebuilding Society
Provides loans to social enterprises in London.
www.londonrebuilding.com

INITIATIVES FOR YOUNG PEOPLE

A Glimmer of Hope
Funds enterprising projects for the under 25s, internationally and in the UK.
www.aglimmerofhope.org

Changemakers
Encourages young people to take the initiative and tackle issues they are concerned about.
www.changemakers.org.uk

Millennium Award winners
Examples of inspiring individuals throughout Britain, and what they have done with their Millennium Award.
www.starpeople.org.uk

Prince's Trust
The Trust's Enterprise Works scheme offers paid work and training for 16-18 year olds, supporting local enterprise.
www.princes-trust.org.uk

MEDIA

'Changing Places'
BBC Radio 4 series featuring 'social entrepreneurs' in Britain whose work is transforming their area.
www.bbc.co.uk/radio4/science/changingplaces

EMES Project
European-wide research into social enterprise.
www.emes.net

'How to Change the World'
Examples of social entrepreneurs from around the world, featured in one handy book.
www.howtochangetheworld.org

Social Enterprise Coalition
Produces a range of publications and links covering social enterprise activity in the UK.
www.socialenterprise.org.uk

Social Enterprise London
Publishes a range of books providing an overview of social enterprise and information on particular areas and fields of activity in the capital.
www.sel.org.uk

Social Enterprise Magazine
Weekly magazine with articles on social enterprise and regeneration in the UK.
www.socialenterprisemag.co.uk

Social Enterprise: A strategy for success
UK government line for supporting social enterprise.
www.dti.gov.uk/socialenterprise

OTHER ORGANISATIONS

Enterprising Solutions Award
National annual award for social enterprise, supported by the DTI Small Business Service, with Social Enterprise magazine.
www.enterprisingsolutions.org.uk

Scarman Trust
Provides practical assistance to local people to bring about change from within communities.
www.thescarmantrust.org

Startups
Site dedicated to everything you need to know about starting up and running your business.
www.startups.co.uk

The Cat's Pyjamas
Training for people developing
social enterprises, run by the
successful Furniture Resource
Centre in Liverpool.
www.the-cats-pyjamas.com

Upstarts Awards
Annual award scheme for
social enterprise and social
entrepreneurs, run by the New
Statesman magazine.
www.newstatesman.co.uk/
upstarts

World in Need
Grant maker investing in the
development of the ideas and
organisations inspired by social
entrepreneurs.
www.world-in-need.org.uk

SOCIAL ECONOMY THINKTANKS

Demos
Independent thinktank that
has published several reports
promoting more enterprising and
entrepreneurial approaches.
www.demos.co.uk

New Economics Foundation
Independent thinktank that
publishes good practice on
social enterprise and community
economic activity.
www.neweconomics.org

Smith Institute
Independent thinktank focusing
on the changing relationships
between social values and
economic imperatives.
www.smith-institute.org.uk

TRAINING

**Centre for Economic
and Social Inclusion**
Provides training that aims
to make organisations better
informed about both policy and
practical day-to-day operational
issues.
www.cesi.org.uk

Directory of Social Change
Provides practical training courses
for voluntary and community
organisations.
www.dsc.org.uk

Learning and Skills Council
Develops and implements
government training. Gateway
to 47 local offices across England
that works with community
groups to provide local training.
www.lsc.gov.uk

**Social Enterprise Training
and Support**
Web-based information resource
to help you find appropriate
training on social enterprise. Also
hosts events and news.
www.setas.co.uk

School for Social Entrepreneurs
Offers hands-on training
programmes for those already
working in social enterprises, and
for those new in the sector.
www.sse.org.uk

Scottish Enterprise
Offers a variety of programmes
designed to give you a valuable
lead over your competitors,
through initiatives such as
Skillseekers and Modern
Apprenticeships
www.scottish-enterprise.com

UK UNIVERSITIES

**Judge Institute,
Cambridge University**
Masters in Community Enterprise.
Part-time qualification for
people working in regeneration
organisations, developed with the
Development Trusts Association.
www.jims.cam.ac.uk

**Skoll Centre for Social
Entrepreneurship, Oxford**
MBA in social entrepreneurship
A global centre for social
entrepreneurship, carrying out
research and education.
www.sbs.ox.ac.uk/html/faculty_
skoll_about.asp

**Social Enterprise Unit,
Heriot Watt University**
Research, consultancy and
good practice to support the
development of social enterprise.
www.sml.hw.ac.uk/
socialenterprise

University of East London
MA/Postgraduate Diploma/
Certificate in Social Enterprise
Qualification for people interested
in social enterprise, developed
with Social Enterprise London.
www.uel.ac.uk

FOR MORE INSPIRATION...

Young Social Enterprise is a magazine packed with stories about dynamic young social entrepreneurs, and the people that work with them.

GET YOUR FREE DOWNLOAD NOW!

www.socialenterprisemag.co.uk

UMBRELLA BODIES

Community Action Network
Online network of social entrepreneurs throughout the UK.
www.can-online.org.uk

Councils for Voluntary Service in Scotland
The organisation that supports, promotes and develops local voluntary and community action.
www.cvsscotland.org.uk

Development Trusts Association
National network of development trusts and community-owned and -led organisations that cultivate enterprise and build assets.
www.dta.org.uk

England: Business Link
National service that provides help and advice on all aspects of setting up and runing a business, whether you're a sole trader or a business with 250 employees.
www.businesslink.org

National Association of Councils for Voluntary Service
Umbrella body for local volunteering centres, with offices UK-wide.
www.nacvs.org.uk

Senscot
Scottish network of social entrepreneurs.
www.senscot.net

Small Business Service
Seeks to promote small businesses by working with others within government and with people in the private and voluntary sectors. Runs regional networks of advice centres run by local providers for small business.
www.sbs.gov.uk

Social Enterprise Coalition
National membership coalition representing the interests of social enterprises.
www.socialenterprise.org.uk

Social Enterprise London
Membership and support network for social enterprises in London.
www.sel.org.uk

Social Enterprise Unit
Government department promoting social enterprise within the Department of Trade and Industry.
www.dti.gov.uk/socialenterprise

Social Firms UK
National network, information and support for companies set up to create employment for disabled people.
www.socialfirms.co.uk

■ **National Council for Voluntary Organisations**
www.ncvo-vol.org.uk
■ **Scottish Council for Voluntary Organisations**
www.scvo.org.uk
■ **Northern Ireland Council for Voluntary Action**
www.nicva.org.uk
■ **Wales Council for Voluntary Action**
www.wcv.org.uk
National umbrella bodies for charities in England Scotland, Northern Ireland and Wales

VOLUNTEERING

Do-it.org
Online databases of volunteering opportunities across the UK.
www.do-it.org.uk

Northern Ireland Volunteer Development Agency
Aims to point people in the right direction and provide useful information for those interested in becoming volunteers.
www.volunteering-ni.org

Timebank
A national volunteering campaign raising the awareness about giving time through voluntary work, inspiring a whole new generation of volunteers.
www.timebank.org.uk

Volunteering England
Promotes volunteering across the UK, with a news wire, a database of organisations and advice.
www.volunteering.org.uk

Volunteering Wales
Advice and listings for volunteering in Wales.
www.volunteering-wales.net

OVERSEAS
DEVELOPMENT

AFTER THE WAVE

IT WAS one of the world's worst-ever natural disasters. But it was after the December 2004 tsunami had retreated that the real battle began: to help hundreds of thousands of survivors who had lost their families, their homes and their livelihoods, and who faced an immediate future of life-threatening hunger and disease.

Help the Aged and HelpAge International worked with partners in India and Sri Lanka to provide emergency relief, and then to ensure that vulnerable older people were able to get the food and shelter they needed. **JOHN COBB**'s photos tell the story of that relief effort, painting a moving picture of lives changed.

In the scrum for food and aid in the immediate aftermath of the tsunami, frail older people were often pushed aside and left with nothing. Help the Aged installed a token system to ensure that every older person could claim their share, and didn't have to fight for their lives. In the months following the wave, the charity began work to rebuild communities, and

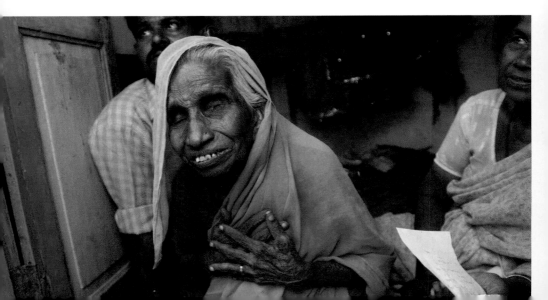

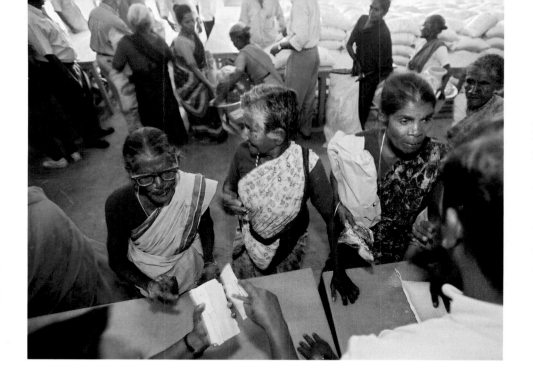

empower the older people affected. It helped older people establish small fishing, cooking and basket-weaving businesses, and provided goats, farm equipment and small cash loans. Small older people's committees were established, to make sure their voices were heard as villages were rebuilt. ▶

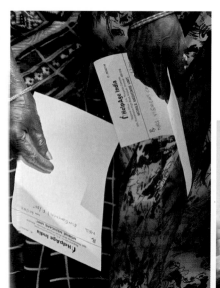

Photographer John Cobb was commissioned by Help the Aged.

→**Help the Aged**
www.helptheaged.org.uk

→**HelpAge International**
www.helpage.org

HEAD OF CAMPAIGNS

Name: James Lloyd
Age: 27

What makes your job so ethical? I'm head of campaigns at People & Planet, which aims to create a just and sustainable world. We do this by involving students in campaigns on issues of poverty, human rights and the environment. We run the largest student campaign network in the UK. Our analysis recognises the way in which these issues are interconnected and emphasises the need for addressing their root causes.

Did you do any specific training or qualifications to get this job? After my degree, I was elected as a sabbatical officer in my students' union. I then went on to be National Union of Students National Secretary.

How did you get into this job? I have always been interested in campaigning and was involved with People & Planet as a student – getting paid to do the things I love seemed like a no-brainer!

What does your typical day involve? I'll meet with other NGOs to plan national and international campaigns, brainstorm new ideas with the campaigns team, talk to student groups, read environmental or development reports, and write lots of emails.

What kind of personality is best suited to working in a job like yours? You're often juggling many projects at the same time so you need to be really organised. You also need an interest in global issues and a commitment to youth empowerment, as well as the ability to come up with the ideas to go with that.

What skills and experience do you need to work in this sector? Experience of campaigning and communications is a must. It's useful to have volunteered or worked as an intern in a campaigning or political organisation.

Best things about the job? Waking up each day and rushing into work to campaign on issues I really believe in. The fact that everyone in the office is so friendly and fun is an added bonus.

Any top tips for someone wanting to get into this work? Get involved with campaigning organisations and take part – that's how you make a difference. ▶

→**People & Planet**
t. 01865 245 678
e. people@peopleandplanet.org
www.peopleandplanet.org

FIRST AID

ELEANOR STANLEY goes behind the scenes to see how frontline international development workers respond to a global emergency.

Photo: John Cobb/Help the Aged

THE SOUTH Asian earthquake was the biggest natural disaster of 2005, with a death toll exceeding 75,000 and more than three million people left homeless. Most of us know something about the massive relief effort, thanks to the dramatic TV coverage beamed into our homes. But what is it actually like being involved in an emergency response of this scale, and how easy is it to get involved?

For aid agency staff, a global disaster means a sharp increase in their workload – and adrenalin levels. This can be both exciting and rewarding, but it also means that social engagements and other commitments go out of the window. News of the earthquake broke on a Saturday, and many staff made their way immediately to the office. Some were on a plane to Pakistan within 24 hours.

Nabeel Sarwar, 24, is a fundraiser for Islamic Relief. "With many of our supporters being from the Pakistani community, we knew this disaster would be a big one for us," he says. Nabeel has a Masters in Chemical Engineering but a strong background in fundraising through university. This was his first emergency.

"Suddenly we were doing 15–20 hour days. It can be difficult managing that level of work alongside other commitments such as family life. I was relatively newly married, so this was my wife's first experience of emergency work too. But you place yourselves in the predicament of the people you are working to help, and that puts the practical stress into perspective."

The experience of working in the field can be even more intense. Daniel Mazliah, 26, had been working as media officer for ActionAid for just four months when he was asked to accompany a journalist to Pakistan for a press trip. Daniel qualified as a journalist and worked on a local paper before moving into media work for charities.

"I'd never been to Asia before and I knew I'd see things that were harrowing," he says. "It had a huge impact on me. It was life-changing in so many ways. Professionally, it brought my job to life because I could see for myself what I was working for. It was a massive responsibility but one I was grateful for."

Unfortunately for ethical job seekers, aid work is an extremely competitive area. Experience is vital. "We have a lot of applicants with a theoretical and academic background, but if it's a choice between an MA and practical experience, the practical experience will win," says Lucy Stoner, director of HR for Care International UK.

Sajni Shah, international personnel administrator for the British Red Cross agrees: "We always rate experience higher than qualification. People interested in aid work should do as much volunteering as possible and be prepared for low remuneration in the early part of their careers. International experience is essential, and languages are always a plus."

There is very high demand for experience in technical areas, such as health and midwifery, water and sanitation, capacity building, community mobilisation, construction engineering and disaster management. But more generic skills are valuable too, says Stoner:

"People think about the programme side of relief work – the shelter building, sanitation or psychosocial support. But you also need the support services to recruit staff, deal with logistics and finances, provide IT support and manage projects. A lot of work these days involves recruiting and building the capacity of local people to make sure the projects are sustainable once we go back to the UK."

It's also important to remember that emergency response is just the most visible tip of the work that many aid agencies are carrying out all year round. Many run smaller-scale development projects, which can provide equally valuable experience in a considerably less pressured environment than an emergency.

People working in emergencies tend to describe their work as exhausting but exhilarating, with the adrenalin carrying them through. "I'd definitely recommend this sort of job," says Daniel Mazliah. "It's good to know that you're making a difference rather than lining the pockets of some fatcat shareholder, and because it's such an important event you feel compelled to do your absolute best."

Ann-Marie Wortley, 24

Ann-Marie is a procurement officer for the medical NGO Merlin. After graduating in archaeology, she worked in Peru as a project manager for a gap-year company. On her return, she started volunteering with Merlin in the logistics department and five months later was offered a full-time job.

"The initial task after the earthquake was getting the teams ready to go, with communications equipment, malnutrition tests and water filters. Sometimes it seemed insurmountable – we'd get a call saying they needed a hospital within 48 hours. It's really a case of being able to cope with a lot of information very quickly, and your emotions are channelled by the people around you to get what's needed done."

Sarah Dodd, 30

Sarah is a disaster management officer for the Tearfund. She worked as an administrator for Tearfund for four years before doing an internship with the Community Rural Health Project in India, and returned to the Tearfund as a public health co-ordinator in Afghanistan and Pakistan. After the South Asian earthquake, she took a role co-ordinating Tearfund's relief effort, and went to Pakistan the following month. "Any development work can be difficult at times, but when you see whole cities smashed and smelling of death, that's very stark," she says. "Emergencies work can seem very sexy, so it's important to find out what your motivation is. If it's just glory, you'll be disappointed because of a lot of it is quite mundane. You need a real degree of self-awareness." ▶

→**ActionAid**
www.actionaid.org.uk

→**British Red Cross**
www.redcross.org.uk

→**Care International**
www.careinternational.org.uk

→**TearFund**
www.tearfund.org.uk

→**Merlin**
www.merlin.org.uk

→**Islamic Relief**
www.islamic-relief.com

FIGHTING FOR SURVIVAL

Kali Mercier works for Survival International, defending the rights of indigenous tribes in Botswana. As NGOs come in for ever closer scrutiny, she tells **PAUL ALLEN** about the ethical challenges of her work.

THE CENTRAL Kalahari game reserve is a safari junkie s dream. Covering an area the size of Switzerland, its vast plains are home to some of the world's most incredible wildlife. But when Kali Mercier tears through the reserve in a 4x4, she isn't scouting for lions or giraffe. The young Kiwi is busy ferrying tribal people to and from the witness stand. Despite the breathtaking surroundings, she spends most of her time in Botswana indoors, holed up in hot, dusty courtrooms.

A research assistant for Survival International, Kali swapped New Zealand for the UK back in 2003, but it is the world's second largest game reserve that now occupies her every waking hour. Survival campaigns on behalf of threatened indigenous peoples around the world. Since joining the charity as an intern in January 2004, Kali has been working on a legal case to stop the Botswana government evicting two ancient Bushmen tribes from the Central Kalahari.

I meet Kali at Survival's central London headquarters, where she has just flown in from Botswana. Two Bushmen are sleeping in the office next door. Tomorrow she will accompany them to Sweden to collect a Right

Livelihood award – dubbed the alternative Nobel Prize – for "resistance against eviction from their ancestral lands, and for upholding the right to their traditional way of life".

Kali fills me in on the struggle. The Gana and Gwi tribes have been living in the Central Kalahari for thousands of years. But in the last decade, most of the 2,000 Bushmen have been forcibly relocated by the government into makeshift camps outside of the reserve. There they face many previously unknown social problems and diseases, such as HIV/AIDS, prostitution and alcoholism. They have also been banned from going back into the reserve, although many have tried – with dire consequences. Several have been tortured and imprisoned, a ban on hunting or gathering food inside the Central Kalahari has seen at least one woman die of starvation.

Survival is helping the Bushmen to fight their government in court, and have called for a boycott on tourism and local diamonds – there has been a major find under their land, and Survival accuses diamond corporation De Beers, which has acquired the mining rights, of colluding with the government's eviction policy. De Beers strongly deny this, insisting the relocations have "nothing to do with diamonds".

On the surface, Survival's ethical credentials appear impeccable. But recently, voices from within Botswana have cast doubt over the charity's claim to the moral high ground. In late 2005, two leading Botswana NGOs working with Bushmen accused Survival of deliberately overstating the oppression of the tribespeople – arguing that its combative approach has actually made life harder for them. They claim Survival's antagonism of the Botswana government has led to an even fiercer crackdown on the tribes.

If these accusations had come from the government, there would be little surprise. The ruling Botswana Democratic Party has always resented Survival's presence in its country, says Kali.

"They really hate the fact that we're white and we come from abroad. They feel we're part of the 'colonialist machine' against them. But we feel we can't stop just because we're from abroad."

Their case, she claims, is also bogus. The government says the evictions are necessary to protect wildlife in the reserve – it argues the Bushmen no longer live their traditional, self-sustainable nomadic lifestyles, instead using guns and off-road vehicles to kill game. Survival flatly rejects this.

But attacks from local NGOs are harder to shrug off. That one of the critical voices is Ditshwanelo, the only human rights organisation in Botswana, has led some international media – including the BBC – to question Survival's intervention in the former British colony. Suddenly the charity has seen itself portrayed as an unwanted outsider meddling in matters it doesn't fully understand.

This is a thorny issue for all charities and international development organisations, especially those coming from the rich, northern hemisphere to 'help' their poorer, southern neighbours. To what extent should a foreign organisation get involved in another country's domestic life? How can it possibly know what is best?

Kali looks downcast. "It does give you a blow when you get that kind of criticism," she says. "You sit back and think, 'Are we doing the right thing?' There'd be something wrong if you didn't.

"But every time I question it and ask the Bushmen if the NGOs are saying anything worthwhile about the campaign, they say, 'No – you must continue!'

The tribespeople argue that even the NGOs have ulterior motives for not wanting them empowered. They allege that Botswana development organisation Kuru is in the payroll of De Beers, and that Ditshwanelo is "fully in bed with the government".

Both organisations strongly refute these allegations. Kuru accepts that it has received funding from De Beers, but insists it is working with the diamond company "to make sure that the company will not exploit the (Bushmen) communities". Ditshwanelo says it, too, is "not convinced that diamonds are the reason for the relocation of the Bushmen" and argues that past negotiations have demonstrated "the potential strengths of discussion and co-operation between the citizens and the government of Botswana". It adds that as a local organisation – unlike Survival – it fully understands the broad cultural context of the tribesmen's struggle.

Despite her conviction in Survival's actions, Kali admits she has been especially conscious of not coming across like an interfering outsider.

"When I first went to Botswana, I was quite nervous," she says. "I didn't want the Bushmen to think I was some white upstart from across the ocean who had come to tell them how to do things. But it was never like that – they were really welcoming."

Survival faces another ethical problem too. Its call for a tourism boycott is harming people's livelihoods in Botswana – one of the poorest countries in the world. How can a charity justify wilfully damaging the local economy?

"We're a small organisation and there are very few things we can do," sighs Kali. "And if it does have an effect on tourism in Botswana, the government can easily end the campaign tomorrow by letting the Bushmen go home.

Ultimately, what they're doing is so appalling that it justifies this action."

Kali never intended to work for a human rights organisation. After a law degree, she took a Masters in International Development, but decided against a career in the sector. "When I was studying, I got quite depressed about development because so many projects fail," she says. "I was also a bit worried about going to communities and 'helping' people." Plans for a career in diplomacy were also short-lived when she realised she would have to change her opinion with each new government.

At Survival, she says, her work is all about empowering the local tribespeople to help themselves. It is also a close-knit organisation with little management hierarchy (Survival currently employs 30 full-time staff) – and if she's interested in a particular campaign, she can usually get involved. Even her job title – research assistant – doesn't reflect the diversity of her everyday work: from writing press releases and researching legal documents for the case, to flying out to Botswana to report on the condition of the Bushmen. It's a demanding job, but even if the future of the Gana and Gwi tribes remains far from certain, there have been plenty of moments to treasure along the way.

"I remember one old man coming up to me in the settlement and saying, 'It's amazing that a little girl like you comes all the way from across the world to help us," she smiles. "That's an incredible thing to hear." ▶

→**Survival International**
www.survival-international.org

→**Ditshwanelo**
www.ditshwanelo.org.bw

→**Kuru**
www.kuru.co.bw

PROGRAMME CO-ORDINATOR, INDONESIA

Name: Henny Ngu
Age: 29

So, what do you actually do? I work with CAFOD projects in and around Indonesia. I work with local organisations in Aceh – the earthquake and tsunami-affected province of Indonesia – by supporting and strengthening their work with Acehnese communities. Our partner organisations work on issues like humanitarian aid provision, reconstruction and longer-term development work.

What makes your job so ethical? This job contributes towards the wider efforts of helping people in need, wherever they are in the world. The ethical challenge is ensuring that by providing aid, we don't cause more dependency, but stronger, independent and progressive communities.

Did you do any specific training or qualifications to get this job? I took short training courses on facilitation skills, project management and financial management, which proved very useful. I've also taken French and Arabic language lessons.

How did you get into this job? My interest began from volunteering work at a shelter for homeless people and a school for disabled children. Since I graduated, I've worked with not-for-profit organisations in a number of countries, including the USA, France, UK, East Timor and Sudan.

What kind of personality is best suited to working in a job like yours? You'll encounter different working styles and approaches, so it is important to have strong intercultural awareness and interpersonal skills. It helps to have an appreciation for the country you're going to, and the willingness to learn about the culture and context that affect the communities you're working with.

What are the most challenging things about your job? The scale of work can be very large, set within complex and ever-changing contexts that are beyond the control of not-for-profit organisations. At times, the work you do can feel like a drop in the ocean.

Any top tips for someone wanting to get into this work? Get as much voluntary experience as possible – preferably a mixture of working in your own local community, with other ethnic groups, and overseas. It's important to get an insight into how communities work, the kinds of issues faced, and the ways these are addressed and resolved. ❱

→**CAFOD**
t. 020 7733 7900
e. cafod@cafod.org.uk
www.cafod.org.uk

PA AND FUNDRAISER

Name: Eileen Veitch-Clark
Age: 25

So, what do you actually do? For three days a week I work with the director and deputy director of the Fairtrade Foundation, sorting out travel itineraries, co-ordinating diaries, drafting letters and so on. For the other two days I'm a fundraiser, putting in applications to trusts and foundations.

What makes your job so ethical? If you see the Fairtrade mark on a product, you can be sure that the farmer who produced it was paid a fair price and worked under decent conditions. We work to bring more businesses into Fairtrade and to raise awareness among the public. The more demand we create in the UK, the more producers can benefit – simple as that!

How did you get into this job? I identified that I wanted to be part of the fair trade movement, so volunteered for the day and never left! I moved to London, worked as a volunteer for six months, got a part-time job and then became full time. Being a volunteer in London is financially very difficult but ultimately it worked out brilliantly.

What does your typical day involve? Being a PA is more challenging and varied than people might think. I've learned a huge amount from working with the directors here. Fitting in the fundraising work is not easy when there's so much else to be done – everyone's stretched. That's the reality of working in a charity with limited resources. But people care about their work and are willing to go the extra mile, which creates a great working environment.

What's the most memorable experience you've had in this job? Hearing a cotton producer from India give a very eloquent speech, standing on stage alongside the Secretary of State for International Development, at the launch of Fairtrade certified cotton.

What are your plans for the future? I've just come back from visiting our international umbrella body, FLO, in Germany and I'm feeling very inspired to work within Fairtrade labelling elsewhere in the world – Costa Rica is my current favourite!

Any top tips for someone wanting to get into this work? Volunteering is the best way to understand the sector and make yourself known. Let your passion for the cause shine through. ▶

→**Fairtrade Foundation**
t. 020 7405 5942
e. mail@fairtrade.org.uk
www.fairtrade.org.uk

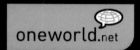

PROGRAMME DIRECTOR, IRAQ

Name: Matthew Wilson
Age: 29

So, what do you actually do? I oversee and manage the planning, implementation, monitoring, evaluation and reporting of War Child UK's programmes in Iraq. We work with children adversely affected by war and conflict, to promote a more secure and protective environment for them and those they depend on.

How did you get into this job? I started out pursuing a legal career then opted for project management in the commercial sector. Three years ago I tried unsuccessfully to get into the development sector. The break came after I invested a couple of years in doing my MSc in Development Management. I also volunteered with international NGOs, which helped me get a better understanding of the sector. I joined War Child as a livelihoods programme manager after being recommended to War Child by another NGO I was doing consultancy work for.

What does your typical day involve? Remotely managing the programmes from Kuwait – emailing and phoning the team in Iraq, meeting with donors, developing materials and guidelines for implementation, security planning, and researching relevant reports on Iraq.

What kind of personality is best suited to working in a job like yours? A calm, resilient, committed, adaptable personality with a strong can-do, problem solving mentality and an appetite for learning.

What's the ideal route in? Opportunities open up if you volunteer, and opportunities exist to volunteer everywhere. Consider turning up in a developing country – things happen when you're on the ground. The overseas development experience that employers look for means more than paying for an expensive gap-year project. Small NGOs will often give volunteers more responsibility, experience and insights than a large one. If you have a Masters, don't expect it to differentiate you from other applicants. Demonstrate you can implement projects effectively. Good intentions or an intellectual understanding is not enough.

Any top tips for someone wanting to get into this work? Be responsible in your ambitions – people's lives will be seriously affected if you get out of your depth and things go wrong. Appreciate that development is incredibly complex. Spend some time working with a local organisation 'in country'. ▶

War Child UK
t. 020 7916 9276
e. info@warchild.org.uk
www.warchild.org.uk

THINK
AGAIN

From top, left to right: Carol Dolby, Naida Begum, Grant Fear, Colin Kirkwood

YOU DO WHAT?

Tortured animals, smelly canals, drugs and crime. Someone's got to deal with it, but not you, right? **HUGH REILLY** and **KATIE TOMS** meet those who do. And they discover that some jobs are far more rewarding that you might think.

ANIMAL RESCUE

Colin Kirkwood, 46, works as an inspector for the RSPCA, investigating animal cruelty, neglect and abuse in the east Kent area, and nursing the animals he has rescued back to health.

The bulk of Colin's work involves investigating animal cruelty, visiting sites where animal neglect is suspected. A typical day might see him visit a home, farmland or even wildlife sites, issuing animal welfare orders where he judges that animals have been placed in possible danger by their owners.

"Thankfully the majority of my time is spent advising people so that the animal doesn't suffer," says Colin.

"Unfortunately with the other five percent we are forced to act."

The RSPCA has the legal basis to rescue animals subjected to unnecessary suffering, which it can then remove to a safe haven and nurse back to health. Colin admits that this part of the job can be very tough indeed, especially with some of the neglect he sees.

In one case, Colin rescued a kitten that had been appallingly abused by a 15 year-old boy. "I think the cat probably used many of its nine lives that day, but it still survived – and survived remarkably well given the circumstances," he says.

Colin joined the

RSPCA five years ago, after completing its intensive seven-month course to become an inspector.

But, he says, his job isn't for everyone. "It is an extremely worthwhile, beneficial job – you get so much from it, but you've really got to be committed."

HANDS ON

Carol Dolby, 43, is a care assistant at St Cecilia's Cheshire Service, a nursing home in Bromley run by the Leonard Cheshire charity for disabled people.

Carol works with 30 residents with particularly complex disabilities, supported by nurses. Her daily tasks include helping the residents with showering and bathing, feeding and toileting, as well as recreational activities such as art and sewing.

Carol says the more hands-on aspects of the job are not as bad as people think.

"Toileting and washing is unappealing, but it is a small part of the job. It's rewarding to be able to help them achieve a better quality of life. The worst part of the job is actually watching the residents deteriorate."

Carol left school to work in an office job, and soon after had children. She was a full-time mother of six sons before joining St Cecilia's just over six years ago as a bed-maker. She then switched to being a carer, and worked up to being a team leader, which she now does five days a week, full time.

"As I got to know the residents, I felt it could be more rewarding caring for them. I was very nervous in the beginning, so I just did a few shifts a week," she says. "Once I tried it, though, that was it. I loved it."

Carol says her job does take a certain type of person. "You've got to be caring, self-motivated and patient." But she insists that people should not be put off. "Once you get in to the job you find out it's not as mundane as you might think. It's different every day, with constant new challenges."

CLEAN FUTURE

Grant Fear, 37, is canal cleansing supervisor at environmental charity Thames 21. He maintains a 30-mile stretch of the Grand Union Canal in London, and a three mile stretch of towpath in the Ladbroke Grove area.

He picks out anything from shopping trolleys to motorbikes, and once even found some leg and thighbones, which turned out to be human. A particularly difficult thing Grant has to deal with, however, is dead animals.

"Foxes and dogs are probably the worst. They smell so much that getting them out almost makes you sick," he says.

Human waste is also not uncommon. "There's lots of urinating along the towpath, especially when Notting Hill carnival is on. The place just stinks afterwards. A lot of people do number twos down there as well. We don't remove them – we just let nature take its course."

But Grant says that once you get used to the early starts, it is a healthy job with lots of exercise and fresh air. That leads to fewer colds and illnesses.

Grant came to the job after his 15 years living a party lifestyle as a fashion photographer left him out of work and facing debt. He has been with Thames 21 for five years, and is now a supervisor.

To get into this job you need to be an outdoors person with good gardening skills: "It's important to have a love of water and the wildlife around it," Grant says. "You also have to be quite self-motivated, because a lot of the time you're working on your own."

Grant says the best bit of his work is involving the community in their canals, but he gets satisfaction just from seeing a clean canal. "Once you have finished cutting the grass and pruning the roses and spring comes along, it all looks really beautiful."

NOT PORRIDGE

Naida Begum, 34, helps rehabilitate and resettle prisoners at Blakenhurst Prison in Redditch, in the west Midlands, for the charity Nacro.

As a manager of Blakenhurst Offender Rehabilitation and Resettlement Solihull (Borris), Naida overseas a team that works with prolific offenders with three months left to serve on their sentences. All offenders covered by the project are addicted to heroin and crack cocaine.

"It's about helping them stay drug free in custody, and working with them quite intensively for the last three months of their sentence to prepare them for release," says Naida.

A typical day for a Borris caseworker might involve drawing up a plan for a new client, helping an offender with issues that will affect

them on their release such as housing, employment, education, benefits, or engaging in group work with the offenders.

Naida admits that dealing with substance misusers can often be emotionally taxing.

"It is very hard because you have clients who die from overdoses… but you just have to go home and forget about it. It would drive you mad if you had to think about it all the time," she says.

On the other hand, the satisfaction gained from helping an offender rehabilitate back into the community is intensely rewarding.

'You do get successes," says Naida, "They might still be using methadone for a long time to come, but they're looking healthy, they're eating better and not looking like a shell."

But not everyone is capable of doing this job. "You need to be resilient and see the long-term picture because this isn't a short-term job – you're never going to get results in a day," says Naida. ▶

RSPCA
www.rspca.org.uk

Leanard Cheshire
www.leonard-cheshire.org

Thames21
www.thames21.org.uk

Nacro
www.nacro.org.uk

ACCOUNTS ASSISTANT

Name: Tegwen Brickley
Age: 31

So, what do you actually do?
I work in the finance department of the Centre for Alternative Technology, administering the day-to-day sales ledger accounts.

What's so ethical about your job? I'm working for an organisation whose purpose is to inspire and help people learn how to use alternative technologies in their homes and businesses.

Did you do any specific training or qualifications to get this job? I went to FE college as a part-time mature student and did NVQ levels 2, 3 and 4 in the Association of Accounting Technicians (AAT) course.

What kind of personality is best suited to working in a job like yours? Accuracy and attention to detail is really important. You have to be patient and persistent, sometimes spending long periods of time working out why the system doesn't match the bank statements and tracking down errors.

What skills and experience do you need to work in this sector? Previous experience of book-keeping is definitely an advantage, as are AAT or similar qualifications, also a commitment to the aims and objectives of the organisation.

What's the most memorable experience you've had in this job? I started working here just before the centre's 30th anniversary celebrations and joined the party-organising committee. We had a lot of fun organising it – and even more on the day!

Best things about the job? Working for an organisation that is so in tune with my values is really important to me. I believe that financial sustainability is essential for all good projects to fulfil their aims – I'm helping to ensure we meet all the legal requirements and keeping an eye on how much money we are getting and spending.

And the most challenging? Sometimes tasks can feel mundane and repetitive. It is a challenge to stay enthusiastic at those times. It is also difficult when someone persistently fails to pay, knowing that we are a charity and need the money.

Any top tips for someone wanting to get into this work? Get experience through helping local community groups with their book-keeping, definitely get some relevant qualifications. Doing voluntary work with groups or organisations that you support will put you in touch with the right people. ▶

→**Centre for Alternative Technology**
t. 01654 705 989
e. info@cat.org.uk
www.cat.org.co.uk

PROPERTY MANAGER

Name: Zoë Colbeck
Age: 30

So, what do you actually do? I manage four National Trust properties, which receive 90,000 visitors a year. The job is really varied, from preparing budgets and marketing plans to organising jazz festivals and sandcastle competitions.

What does your typical day involve? In the summer I am busy with our events programme and all that goes with that. In the winter we are planning and organising for the next season. There's never a quiet time, which is good as I work better under pressure. It's also important to keep your ears open for grants and, of course, you get all those things that crop up on a daily basis that you haven't budgeted time for.

How did you get into this job? I have been a National Trust volunteer since I was 16. This gave me a good grounding in the variety of The National Trust's portfolio and the individual management required for each property. I was persistent. Once I had decided that I wanted to work for the Trust, I spent some time with a house manager to find out more about her job and what the job titles meant. I also spent some time volunteering as a room steward as I had never done that before. I didn't get the first job I applied for but I phoned up and asked for feedback as I knew I had the right skills – I just need to market myself correctly.

What kind of personality is best suited to working in a job like yours? You need to be a jack of all trades. We always run on a tight budget so you need to be creative and get into things 'Blue Peter-style' sometimes. There is always a solution – you just need to find it! You need to have a positive outlook and be able to work on a lot of things at the same time.

What are the most challenging things about your job? We always have restricted resources, so many ideas may take years to happen. As with any large organisation, there are lots of set policies and procedures, which can be frustrating. I focus on what I can do rather than what I can't.

Any top tips for someone wanting to get into this work? Don't just think about it – do something about it. ❱

→**The National Trust**
t. 0870 458 4000
e. enquiries@
thenationaltrust.org.uk
www.nationaltrust.org.uk

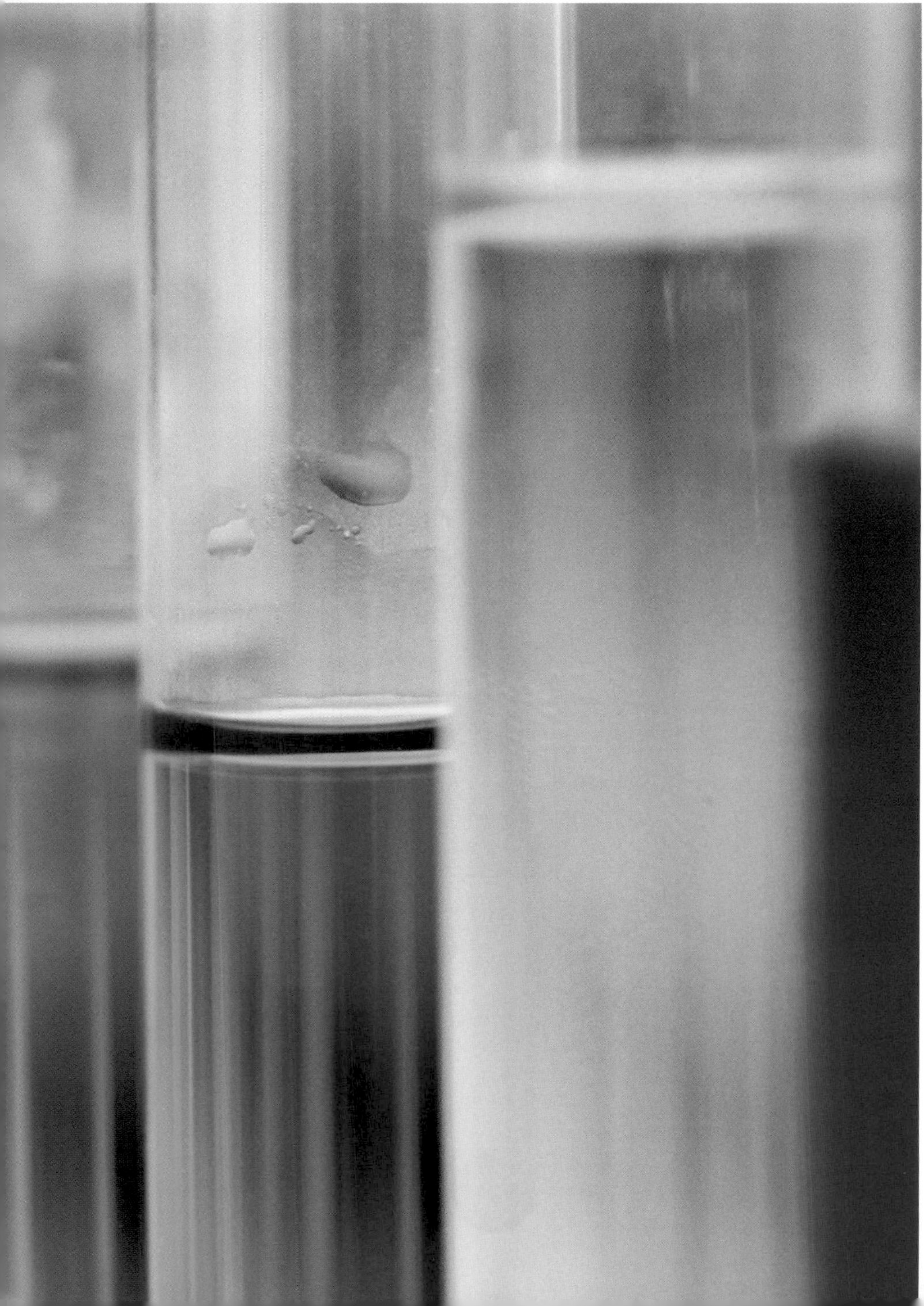

THE RIGHT FORMULA

Science and ethics make an explosive mix, but one that can be achieved in the same career, says **CASPAR VAN VARK.**

SOME SCIENTISTS have long argued that ethical considerations are irrelevant to their work. Science has no room for such emotional distraction, they say. Their work is about research and understanding, not the (mis)application of this new knowledge.

Such a benign view of science is fine if you're talking about clear-cut medical advances, such as the smallpox vaccine. But evaluating the impact of today's scientific community is far more complex. In the past century, for example, it has contributed to many of the planet's biggest problems – like ozone holes, extinctions, toxic spills and global warming.

Some scientists still claim moral immunity, but the tide is turning. There is, in particular, a new generation of science and technology graduates who don't want to leave their ethics at the door when they enter a laboratory.

Scientists for Global Responsibility (SGR) is an independent, UK-based membership organisation of about 850 natural and social scientists, engineers, IT professionals and architects. It is a networking organisation that works to promote ethics in science.

"Ethics are going up the agenda," says Stuart Parkinson, SGR's executive director. "Science has been battered by various criticisms over the years, from the Cold War to genetic modification. Previously, ethics in science was talked about as 'don't lie, don't cheat', but now a government advisory body is putting together a draft ethical code for scientists. There's a growing recognition that ethics have an important part to play."

But how do you get a job as an ethical scientist? Much depends on what you define as 'ethical', but typical areas of work might include clean technologies, climate change, sustainable development and renewable energy.

Unfortunately, while environmental technologies form a growing sector, many of the organisations working specifically in ethical science are quite small, and tend to employ people with experience. For graduates, it's easier to find work with a larger organisation – probably not an overtly ethical one. Big companies can afford to train newcomers, and offer bigger salaries. With a few years' experience, you're more likely to be taken on by a smaller, specialised organisation.

The prospect of working for a huge, global company, even for a few years, might seem horrifying. But even the multinationals have started to wake up to ethics, and by working in one, you can bring about change from within.

That has been Angy Khosla's strategy. She works for ERM, a multinational environmental consultancy. After completing an undergraduate degree in life and environmental sciences, she did an MBA and then an MSc in Environmental Assessment and Evaluation. She now helps big oil and gas companies manage their

social performance.

"I got into this because I think these multinationals have the potential to make a real difference with the access and influence they have in governments," she says. "I was keen to work within those companies to change the way they manage themselves and limit any damage or negative impacts. A lot of their operations are based in poor, isolated parts of the world. When the projects arrive, they raise local expectations because they can bring development. I help manage that process. It's a good way for those corporations to give something back to society."

At the opposite end of the scale is Becky Price, who works for Genewatch, a not-for-profit group that monitors developments in genetic technologies from a public interest, environmental protection and animal welfare perspective. Becky is one of just a handful of employees.

She did a Biology degree and then volunteered with various small environmental groups before arriving at Genewatch, where she manages the website content and is involved in writing and researching the group's campaigns.

Working for a small organisation means Becky feels like she's working at the frontline, and that her efforts make a real difference. "I'm here because I want to do something worthwhile

as opposed to making shareholders a lot of money, or producing another product we don't need," she says.

But to make much headway in her field, she concedes, medical qualifications are practically essential. "If you want to directly challenge science issues on the basis of validity, you need a PhD and lots of experience."

Ethical careers are also spreading far beyond the laboratory – it's not all about research and campaigning. You can be an ethical engineer or architect, working on design and construction to ethical standards.

Aurore Julien is an engineer with Whitbybird, a large engineering company with offices around the UK. Whitbybird has worked on projects such as the Lillywhites building in Piccadilly Circus and the Brighton Dome Concert Hall. Aurore heads the company's small sustainability and renewal team.

"We do sustainability master planning, which covers issues such as windflow, daylight, solar penetration in new developments, waste management, materials selection, water management, and energy efficiency," she says.

There are just five people in her team out of 350 company employees, but Aurore says it's a growing area.

"It's developing quickly. It seems that everyone is thinking about sustainability a bit more now, but it is still very specialised."

As a result, opportunities are thin on the ground and highly competitive. "It's also very technical area, very demanding in terms of maths

and physics," she adds. "You need the right experience."

Aurore studied engineering in France for five years before doing a Masters in Environmental Design and Engineering, and had another job for four years before starting at Whitbybird.

But ethics aren't just for senior management. Even if you're applying for a graduate position, you could work for the solar energy division of a large energy company, for example. Other opportunities are in academia, or the government. The Ministry of Defense is by far the biggest government employer of scientists, but there's also the Sustainability Unit at the Department for the Environment, Food and Rural Affairs (Defra), for example.

Stuart Parkinson at GSR advises jobseekers to first work out their personal 'comfort level'. "If you're very radical you're never going to fit into a multinational," he says. "But companies are taking ethics more seriously."

If more people at entry level start asking the right questions, Parkinson adds, it will make employers think more about their company's ethics. Science graduates are becoming an increasingly rare breed anyway – so if you're going for an interview, don't be afraid to ask about ethical issues. Many employers will expect it of you. And if they find they can't attract young talent, they'll soon change their ways. ◗

→**Scientists for Global Responsibility**
www.sgr.org.uk

→**Gene Watch**
www.genewatch.org

→**Whitbybird**
www.whitbybird.com

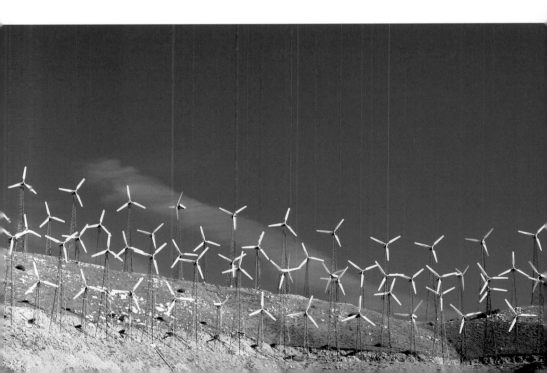

DIRECTOR OF HORTICULTURE

Name: Sue Minter
Age: 56

So, what do you actually do? I'm director of Horticulture at the Eden Project, which means I oversee a 50-strong team of horticulturists – experts in the science of cultivating plants – and scientists who practise 'extreme horticulture' in an old china clay pit in Cornwall that has become a major tourist attraction. When we took it over, it was flooded and had no soil.

What makes your job so ethical? We are trying to change the world by moving towards a more sustainable future in the management of plant resources for human benefit. We like to think that we are about giving power to people to create a better future. Many botanic gardens around the world are doing the same – but we do it with attitude.

What does your typical day involve? I'll normally walk around the site to keep up to speed and talk to staff, followed by meetings and a lot of email (almost all internal as we're such a big site). I may also visit the nursery, which is six miles away. Once a week I work from home to get any concentrated writing done.

What skills and experience do you need to work in this sector? The normal horticultural skills, plus broad plant knowledge, including knowledge of crops, as well as forward planning and people management skills.

What's the most memorable experience you've had in this job? The memory of people bursting into tears because they are moved by something you have successfully communicated in an exhibit. The look of exhilaration on people's faces when they've had their eyes opened to issues that they might be able to affect by the way they choose to behave in the world.

What are the most challenging things about the job? Dealing with changes of mind, direction, and goalposts among management, and getting people to respect different working cultures in such a big organisation.

Any top tips for someone wanting to get into this work? Get a good education in a subject you enjoy, then get good practical skills at a botanic garden. Travel abroad and open your mind. ❱

→**The Eden Project**
t. 01726 811 900
e. info@edenproject.com
www.edenproject.com

CHARITY SPORTS WORKER

Name: John Ellery
Age: 24

So, what do you actually do? I work for Action for Blind People to develop and run sports clubs across the Midlands for visually impaired children. The aim is to give 6-16 year olds the opportunity to learn a range of new sports and skills that they might not otherwise get the chance to do.

What does your typical day involve? There really isn't a typical day. A lot of my work involves meeting and liaising with parents, coaches, facility managers and local sports development officers to expand existing clubs and develop new ones. I'm also involved in delivering visual awareness training, developing tournaments and competitions, building partnerships on a regional level, and coaching activities.

What makes your job so ethical? There is a massive shortage of sports opportunities available for visually impaired people, especially children, so we're trying to satisfy this need.

What kind of personality is best suited to working in a job like yours? It's important to believe in what you're doing. This belief and passion is vital if you're going to wake up at 7am on a Saturday morning to get to a club many miles away.

What's the most memorable experience you've had in this job? Attending a holiday scheme with 20 fearless visually impaired children who completed every possible outdoor activity – zip wires, raft building, climbing and abseiling – while I was left cowering on the side.

Best things about the job? Working with children and really seeing a difference that the clubs make to their lives.

And the most challenging? The struggle we have reaching visually impaired children across the region, many of whom aren't eager to participate in sports activities because of previous bad experiences.

Any top tips for someone wanting to get into this work? Get out there and gain some experience. Ring up your local council or volunteering bureau and find out what opportunities are available to you. Nearly all sports development jobs will require applicants to have some experience – volunteering is an excellent way of getting this. ▶

→**Action for Blind People**
t. 020 7635 4800
e. info@actionforblindpeople.org.uk
www.afbp.org

TIME AT THE BAR

The legal profession is one of the most sought after graduate destinations. But can you keep your ethics intact? **ADRIAN SANDIFORD** reports.

ALL LEGAL work is ethical, according to the Law Society, the regulatory and representative body for the legal profession. And yes, in a way it is. Solicitors in the UK abide by a strict code of legal ethics regulating their professional conduct. But while lawyers undoubtedly acted 'ethically' in the multi-million pound case surrounding Catherine Zeta-Jones and the magazines Hello! and OK!, helping an exceedingly wealthy star sue a magazine over a picture of her eating wedding cake is a far cry from a career making the world a better place.

The good news is that you can choose law as a career, not just for the sake of a career but to work towards positive social outcomes. The opportunities are out there are many and diverse, from working for small community organisations to working in a firm that concentrates on charity clients, or from being an in-house lawyer in an ethical organisation to providing free legal advice to those who can't afford to pay.

The law is a vast arena with many different roles, ranging from legal secretaries to paralegals (lawyers' assistants), explains Isabelle Rolley of the Law Society. "As a trained lawyer the fundamental choice is between two branches of the profession: barrister or solicitor," she says. "Although the distinction has become blurred in recent years, the basic difference is that barristers are self-employed and specialise in representing clients in court, while the solicitor will be employed by a firm and fulfils the role of initial advice and client liaison."

If you choose to qualify as a solicitor – a process that requires you to do a three-year law degree, a one-year post-graduate vocational course called the Legal Practice Course (or two years if you did a non-law degree), and fulfil a two-year training contract with a solicitor's firm – you can use your professional skills to give free help to people in need who cannot afford legal fees.

This is known as 'pro bono' work and is a common practice among solicitors, from the very top city firms down to the smallest high-street lawyers. The Solicitors Pro Bono Group (SPBG) currently helps 20,000 people a year, through the assistance of 2,500 lawyers. In the past year, the SPBG helped 300 small voluntary community groups with their legal issues, through solicitors in private firms offering their services free of charge. "The idea is for lawyers to put back into their community as much as they can," says acting chief executive, Robert Gill.

Gill says that at least a third, and up to a half, of all the solicitors in this country are giving free legal advice on a regular basis, either through the SPBG or from within private practice. But are law firms that spend most of their time helping huge corporates dodge taxes merely salvaging their consciences by indulging in a bit of PR-friendly pro bono?

To address her concern for a firm's ethos, client base and ethical outlook, Stephanie Biden decided to work at Bates Wells & Braithwaite (BWB), a leading law firm that works with the charity and not-for-profit sector.

"Law should have a social purpose," says 25-year-old Stephanie, who has just qualified as a solicitor at BWB, following an English degree at Oxford University, two years of postgraduate legal study, and the two-year training contract. "I wanted to use the skills of a legal career and put those together with the values I had."

Stephanie's lawyer's work with charities, campaign groups and social enterprises includes helping them get set up, advising trustees on their responsibilities, and drawing up agreements with commercial sponsors. "We're helping other people implement their vision for a better society," she says.

If you want to specialise in a certain area of the law – whether that be working with charities, criminal defence of protestors, or human rights – the first opportunity to do so comes when choosing which firm to train at. The study you have to undertake before that point is made up of core subjects that all solicitors, regardless of their future speciality, have to cover. It's the firm you train at, and the work they do, that will begin to shape your specific expertise.

Different firms specialise in different areas. BWB excel in charity law, Bindman & Partners are renowned for their human rights work, while Leigh Day & Co have established close relationships with environmental NGOs. Research the firm's area of work when applying for a training contract to ensure they match your interests.

But places at leading firms like BWB are competitive. Last year 984 people applied for four training contracts. You need to combine academic ability with a proven commitment to your area of interest. While studying for her first degree, Stephanie spent time as a trustee of a student-run charity and took part in a number of sponsored events for good causes.

An alternative to working for a firm with charity or human rights interests is to seek a position as an in-house lawyer at a not-for-profit organisation. This way you can take your valuable legal skills from a private practice to a charity.

After following the traditional solicitor's career path, Luke Joannou decided to move in-house to Cancer Research UK, where he is now senior legal advisor and contracts manager. "I was able to bring my skill set into an organisation that could do some public good. It's my way of giving something back to the community," says Luke, who has been able to use his skills to project manage the legal issues involved in the charity's development of a new scientific research laboratory in Cambridge.

Jobs like those of Stephanie and Luke do not come easily. The study and training required to become a solicitor takes a minimum of six years. Law Society statistics show that fees for the one-year Legal Practice Course range from £5,000 to £8,500. There are, however, potential sources of funding. Some firms will cover the cost of the courses if you secure a training contract with them.

But there are other ways to use the law to achieve social good that don't involve qualifying as a solicitor: you might work or volunteer at a charity that advises people on their problems and the legal issues involved. The Citizens Advice Bureau, for example, helps people get the information they need to address their legal problems. As one of their 21,000 volunteers, you'll receive training to help advise people on all matters of issues.

This approach can be taken further. At Asylum Aid, Carmen Kearney helps people prepare applications for asylum and, if they are turned down, has the experience and accreditation needed to help prepare the case and represent in court. Carmen trained on the job, shadowing people who prepared and represented asylum cases.

To give this sort of legal advice, you have to be recognised by the Office of the Immigration Services Commissioner (OISC), the body responsible for ensuring good practice among immigration advisers. There are three levels of competence that are proved through a series of written examinations.

Carmen also has to be accredited by the Legal Services Commission (LSC) because they provide the legal aid that funds her work in assisting asylum cases. LSC accreditation requires you to pass the requisite test every three years to ensure your competence.

"I wanted to use the law to make an improvement to society, to ensure people's human rights are protected," says Carmen. "I felt a sense of injustice at how the system works. This allows me to use legal skills without having to study areas of the law that are of no interest to me."

So, whichever way you look at it, the ethics of working in law just depend on how you use it. ▶

→**The Law Society**
www.lawsociety.org.uk

→**Solicitors Pro Bono Group**
www.probonogroup.org.uk

→**Bates Wells & Braithwaite**
www.bateswells.co.uk

→**Cancer Research UK**
www.cancerresearchuk.org

→**Citizens Advice Bureau**
www.citizensadvice.org.uk

→**Asylum Aid**
www.asylumaid.org.uk

Transport for London

The TfL Graduate Programme. Where theory becomes reality.

Competitive salary plus 30 days' holiday, free travel in London and other excellent benefits

Helping three million people travel safely around London each day is a big responsibility. And we're not just committed to meeting the needs of the people who travel with us - we're helping make the capital a better place for everyone.

We're currently undertaking a number of initiatives designed to improve our services, promote sustainable transport and reduce the impact we have on the environment. It's a great time to join us, and our current graduates have already discovered how they can help make a difference.

"Recently I've been involved in the road safety programme in Lambeth, and it's fantastic to know that I've played a part in reducing casualty rates in the area." Niaz Choudhury, Civil Engineering Graduate Scheme.

"At TfL we're always trying to make it easier for people to get around. I'm currently looking at wheelchair accessibility in the run up to the Olympics. It's great to work on projects that will actually have an impact on millions of people's lives." Robert Semple, Transport Planning Graduate Scheme.

For more information on these and the other schemes we offer, please visit **www.tfl.gov.uk/graduates** or call **020 8288 5110**.

We want to be as diverse as the city we represent and welcome applications from everyone, regardless of gender, ethnicity, sexual orientation, faith or disability.

MAYOR OF LONDON   Transport for London

DIRECTOR

Name: Dr Stuart Parkinson
Age: 37

So, what do you actually do? I run Scientists for Global Responsibility – an organisation that promotes ethical science, design and technology – in line with the principles of peace, social justice and environmental sustainability. I co-ordinate research, education and lobbying activities on issues in which science, design and technology play an important role.

How did you get into this job? Bizarrely, I started my career as an electronic engineer working for the military on weapons systems. I had fallen for their propaganda and signed up. I very quickly decided this wasn't the best place to be. I went back to university and did a PhD carrying out mathematical modelling of climate change. After some voluntary environmental work I started post-doctoral research on climate policy. I also started doing voluntary work for SGR and was elected onto its Co-ordinating Committee. After five years at Surrey, I moved to Friends of the Earth and co-ordinated their programme on the environment and social justice. Then in early 2003, SGR employed me as its director.

What skills and experience do you need to work in this sector? SGR sits on the divide between the scientific professions and the peace and environmental campaign groups. Hence skills from both sectors are very useful. These include a high level of scientific literacy, good knowledge of policy issues, and good verbal and written communication skills. My dual experience in academia and with campaign groups was very important.

What does your typical day involve? I get to stick my nose into all sorts of things! I can be talking to the press about the latest advances in climate science one day, and helping with research on the military uses of nanotechnology the next.

What kind of personality is best suited to working in a job like yours? One with a high degree of self-motivation, a strong interest in science and its role in society, and a serious commitment to ethical concerns.

What are the most challenging things about your job? The constant need to fundraise and the problem that the forces you're challenging – military and corporate – are so powerful. ▶

→Scientists for Global Responsibility
t. 07771 883 696
e. info@sgr.org.uk
www.sgr.org.uk

RESOURCES

Our unique directory of organisations actively looking for volunteers like you. Published in association with **do-it.org.uk**.

do-it.org.uk is the central place to find volunteering opportunities online.

Its quick and simple postcode search scans more than 700,000 opportunities to volunteer, giving you an instant list of opportunities in your area. The range of opportunities is huge – whatever skills and experience you have, there is something you can do. As well as helping your local community, volunteering is also a great way to meet new people, learn new skills and gain useful experience. ▶

NATIONAL UMBRELLA GROUPS

Northern Ireland Council for Voluntary Action
Umbrella body for voluntary and community organisations in Northern Ireland.
t. 02890 877 777
e. info@nicva.org
www.nicva.org

Northern Ireland Volunteer Development Agency
Aims to promote volunteering and improve the quality of the involvement of volunteers in Northern Ireland.
t. 02890 236 100
e. info@volunteering-ni.org
www.volunteering-ni.org

Scottish Council for Voluntary Organisations
Umbrella body for voluntary organisations in Scotland.
t. 01315 563 882
e. enquiries@scvo.org.uk
www.scvo.org.uk

Volunteer Development Scotland
Works strategically and in partnership to help create an enabling environment for volunteering in Scotland.
t. 01786 479 593
e. information@vds.org.uk
www.vds.org.uk

Volunteering England
Promotes volunteering by working with potential volunteers, volunteers and those who manage volunteers.
t. 08453 056 979
e. information@
volunteeringengland.org
www.volunteeringengland.org

Wales Council for Voluntary Action
Umbrella body for voluntary and community organisations Wales.
t. 08706 071 666
e. help@wcva.org.uk
www.wcva.org.uk

do-it.org.uk works with over 360 Volunteer Development Agencies in England and more than 350 national organisations that provide the volunteering opportunities that fill the database. ◗

FIND YOUR VOLUNTEERING OPPORTUNITY AT do-it.org.uk

VOLUNTEERING ORGANISATIONS

CSV
Offers high quality volunteering, training and professional development opportunities.
t. 020 7278 6601
e. information@csv.org.uk
www.csv.org.uk

Media Trust
Assists the voluntary sector to improve their communications and encourages media professionals to volunteer.
t. 020 7874 7600
e. info@mediatrust.org
www.mediatrust.org

NACVS
The National Association of Councils for Voluntary Service – network of more than 350 CVSs and voluntary infrastructure organisations.
t. 01142 786 636
e. nacvs@nacvs.org.uk
www.nacvs.org.uk

NAVSM
The National Association of Voluntary Service Managers advises health and social care employers about voluntary service managers and promotes training and qualifications for members.
www.navsm.org.uk

Sport England
Creates opportunities for people to start sport, stay in sport and succeed in it.
t. 08458 508 508
e. info@sportengland.org
www.sportengland.org

Student Volunteering England
Increases knowledge, skills and abilities of students, and works in partnership with communities.
t. 0800 0182 146
e. info@studentvolunteering.org.uk
www.studentvolunteering.org.uk

TimeBank
National charity inspiring and connecting people to share and give time by volunteering.
t. 08454 561 668
e. info@timebank.org.uk
www.timebank.org.uk

Youth Action Network
Enables young people to engage with communities, become active and deliver on community projects.
t. 01214 559 732
e. nfo@youth-action.org.uk
www.youth-action.org.uk

ANIMALS

Bat Conservation Trust
The UK's only organisation solely devoted to the conservation of bats and their habitats.
t. 020 7627 2629
e. enquiries@bats.org.uk
www.bats.org.uk

Blue Cross
Provides practical care to animals.
t. 01993 822 651
e. info@bluecross.org.uk
www.bluecross.org.uk

British Union for the Abolition of Vivisection
Campaigns peacefully against animal experiments.
t. 020 7700 4888
e. info@buav.org
www.buav.org

Care For the Wild International
Animal welfare and conservation charity.
t. 01306 627 900
e. info@careforthewild.com
www.careforthewild.org

Cats Protection
Feline welfare charity rescuing and finding new homes for around 60,000 cats and kittens every year.
t. 08702 099 099
e. helpline@cats.org.uk
www.cats.org.uk

Compassion in World Farming
Campaigns to stop factory farming and the long-distance transport of animals worldwide.
t. 01730 264 208
www.ciwf.org.uk

Horses and Ponies Protection Association (HAPPA)
Campaigns for equine welfare.
t. 01282 455 992
e. enquiries@happa.org.uk
www.happa.org.uk

Organisation Cetacea
Promotes the conservation of the marine environment through research, partnership and education.
e. volunteers@orcaweb.org.uk
www.orcaweb.org.uk

PDSA
Promotes responsible pet care and provides free veterinary services for the pets of people needing support.
t. 0800 917 2509
e. volunteers@pdsa.org.uk
www.pdsa.org.uk

RSPB
Works for a healthy environment rich in birds and wildlife.
t. 01767 680 551
e. volunteers@rspb.org.uk
www.rspb.org.uk

RSPCA
Works to promote kindness and prevent cruelty to animals.
t. 0870 3355 9999
e. volbacs@rspca.org.uk
www.rspca.org.uk

Mammal Society
Works to protect British mammals and halt the decline of threatened species.
t. 020 7350 2200
e. enquiries@mammal.org.uk
www.mammal.org.uk

Marine Connection
Works internationally for the care and protection of dolphins and whales.
t. 020 7499 9196
e. info@marineconnection.org
www.marineconnection.org

Mayhew Animal Home
Animal home and humane education and training centre.
t. 020 8969 0178
e. info@mayhewanimalhome.org
www.mayhewanimalhome.org

Monkey Sanctuary Trust
Promotes the welfare, conservation and survival of primates – particularly woolly monkeys.
t. 01503 262 532
e. info@monkeysanctuary.org
www.monkeysanctuary.org

Whale & Dolphin Conservation Society (WDCS)
Global voice for the protection of whales, dolphins and their environment.
t. 08708 700 027
e. info@wdcs.org
www.wdcs.org

WildAid
Works on the ground, across borders and in the marketplace to turn back the tide of extinction.
t. 020 7359 3543
e. acap@wildaid.org
www.wildaid.org/acap

WWF
Works to build long-term solutions to environmental problems for the benefit of people and nature.
t. 01483 426 444
www.wwf.org.uk

THE ARTS

Art House
Works to ensure equal access to the visual arts for disabled people.
t. 01924 377 740
e. info@the-arthouse.org.uk
www.thearthouse.org.uk

Chicken Shed Theatre
Uses drama and music to enable teenagers to learn self-expression through teamwork.
t. 020 8351 6161
e. info@chickenshed.org.uk
www.chickenshed.org.uk

National Art Collections Fund
Campaigns for the widest possible public access to art.
t. 020 7225 4800
e. info@artfund.org
www.artfund.org

October Gallery Trust
Art gallery dedicated to the appreciation of art from all cultures around the world.
t. 020 7242 7367
e. chili@octobergallery.co.uk
www.octobergallery.co.uk

CAMPAIGNS AND INTERNATIONAL DEVELOPMENT

Action Against Hunger
Aims to save lives by combating hunger and malnutrition around the world.
t. 020 7394 6300
e. info@aahuk.org
www.aahuk.org

Action for Southern Africa
Campaigns for peace, democracy and development in Southern Africa.
t. 020 7833 3133
e. actsa@actsa.org
www.actsa.org

Afghanaid
Works for long-term sustainable development in rural areas of Afghanistan.
t. 08712 88 11 44
e. info@afghanaid.org.uk
www.afghanaid.org.uk

Aid to Russia and the Republics
Supports church and humanitarian initiatives in Russia.
t. 020 8460 6046
e. info@arrc.org.uk
www.arrc.org.uk

Amnesty International
Worldwide movement of people who campaign for internationally recognised human rights.
t. 020 7033 1500
e. activism@amnesty.org.uk
www.amnesty.org.uk

Anti-Slavery International
Fights slavery worldwide.
t. 020 7501 8920
e. info@antislavery.org
www.antislavery.org

Azafady
Works on conservation and sustainable development projects in south-east Madagascar.
t. 020 8960 6629
e. mark@azafady.org
www.madagascar.co.uk

Bees for Development Trust
Raises awareness about the value of beekeeping for poverty alleviation.
t. 01600 713 648
e. info@beesfordevelopment.org
www.beesfordevelopment.org

Book Aid International
Works in developing countries to support literacy development, reading, education and training.
t. 020 7733 3577
e. info@bookaid.org
www.bookaid.org

CAFOD
Works to end poverty and make a just world.
t. 020 7733 7900
e. cafod@cafod.org.uk
www.cafod.org.uk

Child Advocacy International
Works to alleviate the suffering of mothers and children in the developing world.
t. 01782 712 599
e. office@caiuk.org
www.caiuk.org

Crisis
Works for the relief of poverty and distress among single homeless people.
t. 08700 113 335
e. volunteering@crisis.org.uk
www.crisis.org.uk

Health Unlimited
Supports poor people in Africa, Asia
and Latin America.
t. 020 7840 3777
www.healthunlimited.org

HealthProm
Works in partnership to improve
healthcare for the most vulnerable in
the former Soviet Union.
t. 020 7284 1620
e. healthprom@healthprom.org
www.healthprom.org

International Health Exchange
Recruits, trains and informs health
professionals to work in areas of
humanitarian need.
t. 020 7233 3116
e. info@ihe.org.uk
www.ihe.org.uk

MAG (Mines Advisory Group)
Works in, and with, communities
devastated by the long-term effects of
human conflict.
t. 0161 236 4311
e. maguk@mag.org.uk
www.magclearsmines.org

Medact
Challenges the barriers to health
worldwide.
t. 020 7324 4739
e. info@medact.org
www.medact.org

Merlin
Provides medical relief to areas of
conflict, natural disaster, disease and
health-system collapse.
t. 020 7065 0800
e. hq@merlin.org.uk
www.merlin.org.uk

Minority Rights Group
Works internationally to challenge
racism around the world.
t. 020 7422 4200
e. minority.rights@mrgmail.org
www.minorityrights.org

Ockenden International
Works to promote self-reliance for
refugees and displaced people.
t. 01483 772 012
e. oi@ockenden.org.uk
www.ockenden.org.uk

One World Trust
Promotes education and research
into the changes required for an end
to poverty, injustice and war.
t. 020 7766 3470
e. info@oneworldtrust.org
www.oneworldtrust.org

Oxfam
Works with others to find lasting
solutions to poverty and suffering
around the world.
t. 0870 333 2700
e. enquiries@oxfam.org.uk
www.oxfam.org.uk

People & Planet
Largest student network in the UK
campaigning on world poverty, human
rights and the environment.
t. 01865 245 678
e. people@peopleandplanet.org
www.peopleandplanet.org

**Phillipine Indigenous
Peoples Links**
Supports indigenous peoples'
organisations to gain recognition and
respect for basic rights
t. 020 7095 1555/07754 395 597
e. info@piplinks.org
www.piplinks.org

Reprieve
Fights for the lives of people facing
the death penalty and other human
rights violations.
t. 020 7353 4640
e. info@reprive.org.uk
www.reprive.org.uk

RESULTS
Works to create the public and
political will to end hunger and the
worst aspects of poverty.
t. 01926 435 430
e. info@results-uk.org
www.results-uk.org

Show Racism the Red Card
Anti-racist charity that aims to use
professional footballers as anti-racist
role models.
t. 01912 910 160
e. ged@theredcard.org
www.theredcard.org

Survival International
Worldwide organisation supporting
tribal peoples.
t. 020 7687 8700
e. info@survival-international.org
www.survival-international.org

Sustain
Campaigns for better food and
farming.
t. 020 7837 1228
e. sustain@sustainweb.org
www.sustainweb.org

CHILDREN

Tackle Africa
Works to stop the spread of
HIV/AIDS in Africa via the platform
of football.
t. 020 7738 2899
e. info@tackleafrica.org
www.tackleafrica.org

The Global Disaster Relief Fund
Helps those who need it most in the
event of a disaster.
t. 020 7629 8456
e. info@gdrf.org.uk
www.gdrf.org.uk

Adopt a Minefield UK
Engages individuals, community
groups and businesses to resolve the
global landmine crisis.
t. 020 7471 5580
www.landmines.org.uk

Tibet Foundation
Works to create greater awareness of
Tibetan culture and the needs of the
Tibetan people.
t. 020 7930 6001
e. office@tibet-foundation.org
www.tibet-foundation.org

Tourism Concern
Campaigns for fairly traded and
ethical tourism.
t. 020 7133 3330
e. info@tourismconcern.org.uk
www.tourismconcern.org.uk

Barnardo's
Works with the most vulnerable
children. helping them transform their
lives and fulfil their potential.
t. 020 8550 8822
e. dorothy.howes@barnardos.org.uk
www.barnardos.org.uk

**British Institute for Brain Injured
Children**
Enables parents of children with
learning difficulties to provide their
children with extra help.
t. 01278 684 060
e. info@bibic.org.uk
www.bibic.org.uk

Child Care Action Trust
Provides equipment and facilities to
disabled children.
t. 08452 300 195
e. childcareaction@aol.com
www.thechildcareactiontrust.org.uk

Childhood First
Provides services for children and
young people who have suffered
abuse, neglect or deprivation.
t. 020 7928 7388
e. enquiries@childhoodfirst.org.uk
www.childhoodfirst.org.uk

ChildLine
Free, national helpline for children and
young people in danger and distress.
t. 020 7650 3200
e. volenquiries@childline.org.uk
www.childline.org.uk

Children's Kidney Trust
Provides support, care workers,
nursing awards, home visits and
family respite time.
t. 08452 301 640
e. enquiries@
childrenskidneytrust.org.uk
www.childrenskidneytrust.org.uk

**Children's Safety Education
Foundation**
Aims to promote the personal
safety, social, health and citizenship
education of children.
t. 01614 775 122
e. general@
childsafetyeducation.org.uk
www.childsafetyeducation.org.uk

East Anglia's Children's Hospices
Cares for terminally ill children and
their families in East Anglia.
t. 01223 205 180
e. terasa.ford@each.org.uk
www.each.org.uk

KIDS
Provides services for children and
young people who have disabilities or
special needs.
t. 020 7359 3635
e. enquiries@kids.org.uk
www.kids-online.org.uk

Make-A-Wish Foundation
Turns the wishes of children aged
3-18, living with a life threatening
illnesses, into reality.
t. 01276 241 27
e. info@make-a-wish.org.uk
www.make-a-wish.org.uk

COMMUNITY

National Association of Child Contact Centres
Supports neutral meeting places where children of separated families can enjoy contact with family.
t. 08454 500 280
e. contact@naccc.org.uk
www.naccc.org.uk

NSPCC
Specialises in child protection and the prevention of cruelty to children.
t. 020 7825 2500
e. info@nspcc.org.uk
www.nspcc.org.uk

Parentline Plus
Works to recognise and value different types of families, and expand the services available to them.
t. 020 7284 5500
www.parentlineplus.org.uk

Rainbow Trust Children's Charity
Cares for children with a life-threatening or terminal illness and their families.
t. 01372 363 438
e. enquiries@rainbowtrust.org.uk
www.rainbowtrust.org.uk

Sargent Cancer Care for Children
UK wide support of children and young people with cancer, and their families.
t. 020 8752 2892
e. info@sargent.org
www.sargent.org

Save the Children
Fights for children who suffer from poverty, disease, injustice and violence.
t. 020 7012 6400
e. volunteering@savethechildren.org.uk
www.savethechildren.org.uk

Smartchange
Develops and delivers technology solutions to help charities become more efficient and effective.
t. 020 8509 0345
e. info@smartchange.org
www.smartchange.org

SPARKS
Children's charity raising money to fund medical research to help children to be born healthy.
t. 020 7799 2111
e. info@sparks.org.uk
www.sparks.org.uk

Special Kids in the UK
Provides support, information and contact between families of children with special needs.
t. 01932 356 416
e. information@specialkidsintheuk.org
www.specialkidsintheuk.org

Spurgeons Child Care
Helps vulnerable children and families as a practical expression of the Christian faith.
t. 01933 412 412
e. scc@spurgeons.org
www.spurgeonschildcare.org

Businessdynamics
Gives young people the skills and knowledge they need to be effective in the workplace.
t. 020 7620 0735
e. info@businessdynamics.org.uk
www.businessdynamics.org.uk

Citizens Advice
The national association of Citizens Advice Bureaux.
t. 020 7833 2181
www.citizensadvice.org.uk

Crime Concern
Works with local partners to prevent crime and create safer communities.
t. 01793 863 500
e. info@crimeconcern.org.uk
www.crimeconcern.org.uk

Crimestoppers Trust
Helps to solve crimes.
t. 0800 555 111
www.crimestoppers-uk.org

Criminon
Provides crime prevention and rehabilitation programmes to people in need.
t. 01342 316 042
e. susan@criminon.org
www.criminon.org

Groundswell UK
Supports a wide range of self-help initiatives led by homeless and socially excluded people.
t. 020 7737 5500
e. info@groundswell.org.uk
www.groundswell.org.uk

DISABILITY

Liberty
Works to protect civil liberties and promote human rights in England and Wales.
t. 020 7403 3888
e. info@liberty-human-rights.org.uk
www.liberty-human-rights.org.uk

London 21
Promotes, supports and networks for a greener, healthier, and more sustainable Greater London.
t. 020 8968 4601
e. office@london21.org
www.london21.org

Nacro
Makes society safer by finding practical solutions to reducing crime.
t. 020 7582 6500
e. helpline@nacro.org.uk
www.nacro.org.uk

One Plus One
Strengthens couple and family relationships by putting research into practice.
t. 020 7841 3660
e. info@oneplusone.org.uk
www.oneplusone.org.uk

PEP Trust
Involves local people in the development, management and delivery of local activities and services.
t. 01618 773 223
e. info@pep.org.uk
www.pep.org.uk

Prisoners Abroad
Provides support to Britons detained overseas, their families and friends, and released prisoners.
t. 020 7561 6820
e. info@prisonersabroad.org.uk
www.prisonersabroad.org.uk

Prisoners' Families & Friends Service
Provides support and information for families and friends of people in prison.
t. 020 7403 4091/9359
e. info@prisonersfamiliesandfriends.org.uk
www.prisonersfamiliesandfriends.org.uk

SSAFA Forces Help
Helps serving and ex-service men, women and their families, in need.
t. 08451 300 975
e. info@ssafa.org.uk
www.ssafa.org.uk

St John Ambulance Library Service
National library service for people in hospitals, residential care homes and day centres.
t. 0870 104 950
e. library-service@nhq.sja.org.uk
www.sja.org.uk

Tolerance in Diversity
Youth-led charity that promotes good relationships in the community.
t. 020 7515 3555
e. li@tid.org.uk
www.tid.org.uk

Training For Life
Contributes to a more inclusive society by empowering people with self-belief.
t. 020 7444 4000
e. info@trainingforlife.org
www.trainingforlife.org

Women's Aid
Works to end domestic violence against women and children.
t. 01179 444 411
e. info@womensaid.org.uk
www.womensaid.org.uk

Action For People
Aims to enable blind and partially sighted people to enjoy equal opportunities.
t. 020 7635 4800
e. info@actionforblindpeople.org.uk
www.afbp.org

Afasic
Seeks to create better services and provision for young people with speech and language impairments.
t. 020 7490 9410
e. info@afasic.org.uk
www.afasic.org.uk

Anne Lloyd Memorial Trust
Provides services for deafblind, deaf and visually impaired people and their families and friends.
t. 01255 420 595
e. slyvia@toosey.fsnet.co.uk
www.stannesbreaks.org.uk

Back-Up Trust
Supports those paralysed through spinal cord injury.
t. 020 8875 1805
e. admin@backuptrust.org.uk
www.backuptrust.org.uk

Choice Support
Provides a wide range of services for people with learning disabilities.
t. 020 7261 4100
e. choicesupport@choicesupport.org.uk
www.choicesupport.org.uk

DIAL UK
Network of local disability information and advice services run by, and for, disabled people.
t. 01302 310 123
e. informationenquiries@dialuk.org.uk
www.dialuk.info

volunteering made easy

Disabled Living Foundation
Supports people with disabilities, and older people.
t. 020 7289 6111
e. info@dlf.org.uk
www.dlf.org.uk

Elizabeth FitzRoy Support
Provides practical support for adults with all forms of learning disability.
t. 01730 711 111
e. info@efitzroy.org.uk
www.efitzroy.org.uk

Greater London Fund for the Blind
Improves the lives of blind and partially sighted people through education, technology and support.
t. 020 7620 2066
e. info@glfb.org.uk
www.glfb.org.uk

Handicap International UK
Supports disabled people in over 50 countries.
t. 08707 743 737
e. hi-uk@hi-uk.org
www.handicap-international.org.uk

Kith & Kids
Empowers families living with disability to access the services they need.
t. 020 8801 7432
e. projects@kithandkids.org.uk
www.kithandkids.org.uk

Larches Trust
Provides care and opportunities for adults over 19 years of age who have a learning disability.
t. 020 8905 6333
e. enquiries@larchestrust.org.uk
www.larchestrust.org.uk

Leonard Cheshire
Exists to change attitudes to disability and to serve disabled people around the world.
t. 020 7802 8200
e. info@lc-uk.org
www.leonard-cheshire.org

Limbless Association
Information, advice and support for people of all ages who are without one or more limbs.
t. 020 8788 1777
www.limbless-association.org

Mencap
Works with people with a learning disability and their families and carers.
t. 020 7454 0454
e. information@mencap.org.uk
www.mencap.org.uk

Out & About
Provides flexible needs-led services to support disabled children and young people and their families.
t. 08707 705 767
e. admin@out-and-about.org.uk
www.out-and-about.org.uk

RNID
Provides services for deaf and hard of hearing people.
t. 020 7296 8000
e. information@rnid.org.uk
www.rnid.org.uk

Royal London Society for the Blind
Provides services to enable people with a visual impairment to lead independent lives.
t. 01732 592 500
e. workbridge@rlsb.org.uk
www.rlsb.org.uk

Royal National Institute of the Blind
Works for a world where people who are blind or partially sighted enjoy equal rights.
t. 020 7388 1266
e. helpline@rnib.org.uk
www.rnib.org.uk

Scope
National disability organisation focusing on people with cerebral palsy.
t. 020 7619 7100
www.scope.org.uk

Sense
Works with people who have sight and hearing difficulties.
t. 020 7272 7774
e. enquiries@sense.org.uk
www.sense.org.uk

Shaftesbury Society
Provides care and education for adults and children with disabilities.
t. 0845 330 6033
e. info@shaftesburysoc.org.uk
www.shaftesburysoc.org.uk

Spinal Injuries Association
Provides services for spinal cord injured people and their families.
t. 0845 678 6633
e. sia@spinal.co.uk
www.spinal.co.uk

St Dunstan's
Provides an independent future for blind ex-service men and women.
t. 020 7723 5021
e. enquiries@st-dunstans.org.uk
www.st-dunstans.org.uk

Whizz-Kidz
Provides disabled children with customised mobility equipment, training and advice.
t. 020 7233 6600
e. info@whizz-kids.org.uk
www.whizz-kidz.org.uk

ENVIRONMENT

BTCV
Practical conservation charity.
t. 01302 572 244
e. information@btcv.org.uk
www.btcv.org

Earthwatch Institute (Europe)
Conserves the diversity and integrity
of life on earth to meet the needs of
current and future generations.
t. 01865 318 838
e. info@earthwatch.org.uk
www.earthwatch.org

Fairtrade Foundation
Raises awareness and understanding
of the Fairtrade mark, and increases
sales of certified products.
t. 020 7405 5942
e. mail@fairtrade.org.uk
www.fairtrade.org.uk

Friends of the Earth
Inspires solutions to environmental
problems.
t. 020 7490 1555
e. info@foe.co.uk
www.foe.co.uk

Grasslands Trust
Protects and enhance areas of
grassland to benefit wildlife and
people.
t. 01962 861 610
e. jon.walkers@bbc.co.uk

Green and Away
Event venue offering groups and
organisations a natural, eco-friendly
and creative meeting space.
t. 0870 601 198
e. info@greenandaway.org
www.greenandaway.org

GreenNet Educational Trust
Part of the global computer network
for environment, peace, human rights
and development groups.
t. 08450 554 011
e. info@
greenneteducationaltrust.org.uk
www.greenneteducationaltrust.org.uk

Groundwork
Runs regeneration projects, from
small community schemes to major
regional and national programmes.
t. 01212 368 565
e. info@groundwork.org.uk
www.groundwork.org.uk

Grownupgreen
Encourages people to think and act
in ways that protect and improve the
natural environment.
t. 01462 649 547
e. enquiries@grownupgreen.org.uk
www.grownupgreen.org.uk

Kent Wildlife Trust
Aims to secure a better future for the
wildlife of Kent.
t. 01622 662 012
e. info@kentwildlife.org.uk
www.kentwildlife.org.uk

Marine Conservation Society
Protects the marine environment and
its wildlife.
t. 01989 566 017
e. info@mcsuk.org
www.mcsuk.org

National Trust
Works to preserve and protect the
coastline, countryside and buildings
of England, Wales and N. Ireland.
t. 08704 584 000
e. enquiries@thenationaltrust.org.uk
www.nationaltrust.org.uk

Plantlife International
Protects Britain's wild flowers and
plants, fungi and lichens, and the
habitats in which they are found.
t. 01722 342 730
e. enquiries@plantlife.org.uk
www.plantlife.org.uk

Royal Horticultural Society
Advances horticulture and promotes
good gardening.
t. 020 7834 4333
e. info@rhs.org.uk
www.rhs.org.uk

Sustrans
Practical projects encouraging people
to walk, cycle and use public transport.
t. 01179 268 893
e. info@sustrans.org.uk
www.sustrans.org.uk

Thames 21
Works with communities to create
safe and sustainable waterside
environments in London.
t. 020 7248 7171
e. info@thames21.org.uk
www.thames21.org.uk

Thames Explorer Trust
Promotes education about the
Thames and works to improve access
to the river.
t. 020 8742 0057
e. info@thames-explorer.org.uk
www.thames-explorer.org.uk

WaterAid
Sustainable provision of safe
domestic water, sanitation and
hygiene education to the world's
poorest people.
t. 020 7793 4500
e. wateraid@wateraid.org
www.wateraid.org.uk

HEALTH AND SOCIAL CARE

Wilderness Foundation
Protects wilderness areas by educating people about their benefits.
t. 01245 443 073
e. info@wildernessfoundation.org.uk
www.wildernessfoundation.org.uk

Wildfowl and Wetlands Trust
Aims to conserve wetlands for wildlife and people.
t. 01453 891 900
e. enquiries@wwt.org.uk
www.wwt.org.uk

Wildlife For All Trust
Protects endangered wildlife and threatened habitats.
www.wildlifeforall.org

Wildlife Trusts
Works to protect wildlife in towns and the countryside.
t. 08700 367 711
e. enquiry@wildlifetrusts.org
www.wildlifetrusts.org

Woodland Trust
Woodland conservation charity.
t. 01476 581 135
www.woodland-trust.org.uk

Yorkshire Wildlife Trust
Protects vulnerable wildlife of all types – animals, birds and plants – and the places where they live.
t. 01904 659 570
e. yorkshirewt@cix.co.uk
www.yorkshire-wildlife-trust.org.uk

Action against Medical Accidents
Promotes better patient safety and justice for people who have been affected by a medical accident.
t. 020 8688 9555
e. advice@avma.org.uk
www.amva.org.uk

Addaction
Provides support for people with drug and alcohol problems.
t. 020 7251 5860
e. info@addaction.org.uk
www.addaction.org.uk

Alzheimer's Society
UK's leading care and research charity for people with dementia, their families and carers.
t. 020 7306 0606
e. enquiries@alzheimers.org.uk
www.alzheimers.org.uk

Arthritis Care
Gives support, understanding, information and expertise to people with arthritis.
t. 020 7380 6500
e. info@arthritiscare.org.uk
www.arthritiscare.org.uk

Asthma UK
Works to improve the health and well-being of the 5.1 million people in the UK who have asthma.
t. 020 7786 4900
e. info@asthma.org.uk
www.asthma.org.uk

BackCare
Helps people manage and prevent back pain by providing information, promoting self help and funding research.
t. 020 8977 5474
e. info@backcare.org.uk
www.backcare.org.uk

Bell's Palsy Association
Offers support and information to sufferers of Bell's Palsy.
t. 0870 44 45 46 0
e. enquiries@bellspalsy.org.uk
www.bellspalsy.org.uk

Black Health Agency
Charity dedicated to improving the future of black and minority ethnic communities.
t. 08454 504 247
e. info@blackhealthagency.org.uk
www.blackhealthagency.org.uk

Blood Pressure Association
Aims at making a real difference to the 16 million people affected by high blood pressure in the UK.
t. 020 8772 4994
www.bpassoc.org.uk

Breast Cancer Campaign
Funds research that aims to cure breast cancer.
t. 020 7749 3700
e. info@bcc-uk.org
www.breastcancercampaign.org

British Heart Foundation
Leading UK heart research charity, which also provides funding and education.
t. 020 7935 0185
www.bhf.org.uk

British Lung Foundation
Supports people affected by lung disease.
t. 08458 50 50 20
www.lunguk.org

British Red Cross
Provides relief to people in crisis – both in the UK and overseas.
t. 08701 707 000
e. information@redcross.org.uk
www.redcross.org.uk

Brook
Provides free and confidential sexual health advice to people under the age of 25.
t. 020 7284 6040
e. admin@brookcentres.org.uk
www.brook.org.uk

Cancer Research UK
World's largest independent organisation dedicated to cancer research.
t. 020 7121 6699
www.cancerresearchuk.org

Chinese Mental Health Association
Provides Chinese mental health services and represents this issue in the public sphere.
t 020 7613 1008
e. info@cmha.org.uk
www.cmha.org.uk

Crusaid
Funds HIV/AIDS prevention and education projects and supports outpatient clinics and back-to-work projects.
t. 020 7539 3880
e. office@crusaid.org.uk
www.crusaid.org.uk

Depression Alliance
Works to relieve and prevent this treatable condition by providing information and support.
t. 0845 23 23 20
e. information@
depressionalliance.org
www.depressionalliance.org

Eating Disorders Association
Provides information, help and support to people affected by eating disorders.
t. 0870 773 256
e. info@edauk.com
www.edauk.com

Encephalitis Society
Raises awareness and provides a dedicated service to people affected by encephalitis.
t. 01653 699 599
e. support@encephalitis.info
www.encephalitis.info

Haemophilia Society
National charity for people with haemophilia, von Willebrand's and related bleeding disorders.
t. 020 7831 1020
e. info@haemophilia.org.uk
www.haemophilia.org.uk

Headway – the brain injury association
Provides a better quality of life for people with acquired brain injury, their families and carers.
t. 01159 240 800
e. enquiries@headway.org.uk
www.headway.org.uk

Leukaemia Research Fund
The UK's largest charity devoted exclusively to leukaemia and related blood cancers.
t. 020 7405 0101
e. info@lrf.org.uk
www.lrf.org.uk

Marie Curie Cancer Care
Provides free, high quality nursing, giving terminally ill people the choice of dying at home.
t. 020 7599 7777
www.mariecurie.org.uk

Men's Health Forum
Provides an independent and authoritative voice for male health in England and Wales.
t. 020 7388 4449
e. office@menshealthforum.org.uk
www.menshealthforum.org.uk

Mind
Works for people with experience of mental distress in England and Wales.
t. 020 8519 2122
e. contact@mind.org.uk
www.mind.org.uk

Miscarriage Association
Offers support and information to those affected by the loss of a baby in pregnancy.
t. 01924 200 795
e. info@miscarriageassociation.org.uk
www.miscarriageassociation.org.uk

Positively Women
Offers peer support to women living with HIV.
t. 020 7713 0444
www.positivelywomen.org.uk

Prostate Cancer Charity
Provides support, information, and funding research to fight prostate cancer.
t. 020 8222 7622
e. info@prostate-cancer.org.uk
www.prostate-cancer.org.uk

React
Works to improve the quality of life for financially disadvantaged children with potentially terminal illnesses.
t. 020 8940 2575
e. react@reactcharity.org
www.reactcharity.org

Relate
Largest provider of relationship counselling and sex therapy in the UK.
t. 08454 561 310
e. enquiries@relate.org.uk
www.relate.org.uk

do-it.org.uk
volunteering made easy

HOUSING AND HOMELESSNESS

OLDER PEOPLE

Release
Provides services dedicated to meeting the health, welfare and legal needs of drug users.
t. 020 7729 5255
e. ask@release.org.uk
www.release.org.uk

Refuge
Network of safe houses that provides emergency accommodation for women and children in need.
t. 020 7395 7700
e. info@refuge.org.uk
www.refuge.org.uk

Samaritans
Provides confidential emotional support 24 hours a day to anyone experiencing emotional distress.
t. 020 8294 8300
e. admin@samaritans.org
www.samaritans.org

SANELINE
National telephone helpline that raises awareness and respect for people with mental illness.
t. 020 7375 1002
e. london@sane.org.uk
www.sane.org.uk

Sue Ryder Care
Cares for chronically sick and disabled people. Has a specialist centre for neurological conditions.
t. 020 7400 0440
www.suerydercare.org

Terrence Higgins Trust
Delivers health promotion and direct services to people affected by HIV and AIDS.
t. 020 7831 0330
e. info@tht.org.uk
www.tht.org.uk

Bield Housing Association
Provides high quality appropriate housing, care and support services for older people.
t. 01312 734 000
e. info@bield.co.uk
www.bield.co.uk

Broadway
Provides emergency accommodation and support to single people in crisis.
t. 020 7089 9500
e. broadway@broadwaylondon.org
www.broadwaylondon.org

Emmaus
Provides a home and work for previously homeless people.
t. 01223 576 103
e. contact@emmaus.org.uk
www.emmaus.org.uk

NOMAD Homeless Advice and Support Unit
Provides advice and support for homeless people.
t. 01142 636 624
e. director@nomadsheffield.co.uk
www.nomadsheffield.co.uk

Resource Information Service
Publishes books, CD-ROMS and websites for the homeless or disadvantaged people.
t. 020 7939 0641
www.ris.org.uk

Shelter
Campaigns for new laws and solutions to Britain's housing crisis to ensure that everyone has a home.
t. 08454 584 590
e. info@shelter.org.uk
www.shelter.org.uk

St Matthew Housing
Provides good quality supported housing for lonely and vulnerable people.
t. 01284 732 550
e. info@stmatthewshousing.org
www.stmatthewshousing.org

Abbeyfield Society
Set up by groups of local volunteers to provide housing with care for older people throughout the UK.
t. 01727 857 536
e. post@abbeyfield.com
www.abbeyfield.com

Action on Elder Abuse
Aims to prevent the abuse of older people by raising awareness, encouraging education and promoting research.
t. 020 8769 7000
e. enquiries@elderabuse.org.uk
www.elderabuse.org.uk

Age Concern
Promotes the improvement of quality of life for older people.
t. 020 8765 7200
www.ageconcern.org.uk

Contact The Elderly
Organises gatherings for frail, elderly people who live alone.
t. 0800 716 543
www.contact-the-elderly.org

Help the Aged
Fights abuse, age discrimination and pensioner poverty.
t. 020 7278 1114
e. info@helptheaged.org.uk
www.helptheaged.org.uk

Retirement Trust
Furthers the knowledge and welfare of the retired and those approaching retirement.
t. 020 7864 9908
e. info@theretirementtrust.org.uk
www.theretirementtrust.org.uk

SPORT

London Sports Forum for Disabled People
Develops sport and recreation for all disabled people throughout Greater London.
t 020 7354 8666
e info@londonsportsforum.org.uk
www.londonsportsforum.org.uk

Royal Aero Club Trust
National co-ordinating body for Air Sport in the United Kingdom.
t. 01926 332 713
e. secretary@royalaeroclub.org
www.royalaeroclub.org

Sport Relief
Organises sport events for charity.
e. info@sportrelief.com
www.sportrelief.com

SportsAid
Helps aspiring young sportsmen and women.
t. 020 7273 1975
e. mail@sportsaid.org.uk
www.sportsaid.org.uk

Street Football League
Uses sport to transform the lives of underprivileged and socially excluded individuals.
t. 020 7480 4150
www.streetleague.co.uk

YOUNG PEOPLE

Changemakers
Enables young people to facilitate and promote youth-led projects and approaches for peers and adults.
t. 01458 834 767
e. info@changemakers.org
www.changemakers.org.uk

do-it.org.uk
do-it.org.uk is the first, and still the only, national database of volunteering opportunities in the UK.
t. 020 7226 8008
www.do-it.org.uk

Envision
Supports young people to develop the skills, confidence and motivation necessary for positive change.
t. 020 7974 8440
e. vision@envision.org.uk
www.envision.org.uk

Get Connected
Free, confidential phone and email helpline for those up to the age of 25 with any kind of problem.
t. 08088 084 949
e. help@getconnected.org.uk
www.getconnected.org.uk

Girlguiding UK
Provides opportunities for girls and young women to be challenged by new adventures and experiences.
t. 020 7834 6242
e. chq@girlguiding.org.uk
www.girlguiding.org.uk

National Youth Music Theatre
Gives young people the opportunity to participate in all aspects of music theatre.
t. 020 8679 1812
e. enquiries@nymt.org.uk
www.nymt.org.uk

After Adoption
Freephone helpline for young people with a connection to adoption.
t. 01618 394 932
e. admin@talkadoption.org.uk
www.afteradoption.org.uk

Duke of Edinburgh's Award
Provides a challenging and rewarding programme of personal development for young people.
t. 01753 727 400
e. info@theaward.org
www.theaward.org

Outward Bound Trust
Gives disadvantaged young people the opportunity to take part in Outward Bound courses.
t. 01931 740 000
e. enquiries@outwardbound-uk.org
www.outwardbound-uk.org

Scout Association
Helps those aged 6-25 achieve their full physical, intellectual, social and spiritual potential.
t. 020 8433 7100
e. info.centre@scout.org.uk
www.scouts.org.uk

Sea Cadets
Aims to help the personal and social development of young people.
t. 020 7654 7000
e. schq@sea-cadets.org
www.sea-cadets.org

Kids City
Award-winning after-school club providing education and recreation to children aged 4-11.
t. 020 8683 9600
e. info@kidscity.org.uk
www.kidscity.org.uk

volunteering made easy

INTERNATIONAL VOLUNTEERING

TheSite.org
Award-winning advice site for 16 to 24 year-olds.
t. 020 7226 8008
e. feedback@thesite.org
www.thesite.org

Weston Spirit
Provides development programmes for young people whose lifestyles reflect a lack of opportunity.
t. 01512 581 066
e. info@westonspirit.org.uk
www.westonspirit.org.uk

YMCA
Leading Christian charity committed to supporting all young people, particularly in times of need.
t. 020 8520 5599
e. reception@ymca.org.uk
www.ymca.org.uk

Youth2Youth
Helpline run by young people for anyone under the age of 19 years who needs emotional support.
t. 020 8896 3675
e. office@youth2youth.co.uk
www.youth2youth.co.uk

Youth Action Network
Encourages young people to engage with communities, helping them to gain skills and have fun.
t. 01214 559 732
e. info@youth-action.org.uk
www.youth-action.org.uk

Youth At Risk UK
Approach troubled youngsters and teenagers, providing them with a powerful way to reclaim their youth.
t. 01763 241 120
e. christine.i@youthatrisk.org.uk
www.youthatrisk.org.uk

Action for Children in Conflict
Lists vacancies for skilled and experienced people to work on projects in Sierra Leone, Kenya and Tanzania.
t. 01865 821 380
e. info@actionchildren.org
www.actionchildren.org

Challenges Worldwide
Matches volunteers to focused short-term voluntary placements overseas.
t. 08452 000 342
e. enquire@challengesworldwide.com
www.challengesworldwide.com

Concern
Enables poor people to achieve major improvements in lifestyle.
t. 020 7738 1033
e. londoninfo@concern.net
www.concern.net

GapGuru
Volunteering opportunities for people of all ages in India.
t. 08706 091 796
e. info@gapguru.com
www.gapguru.com

Goal
International humanitarian agency dedicated to the alleviation of the suffering of the world's poorest.
t. 020 7631 3196
e. info@goal-uk.org
www.goal.ie

ICYE
Inter-Cultural Youth Exchange UK promotes inter-cultural awareness through overseas volunteering.
t. 08707 743 486
e. international@icye.org.uk
www.icye.org.uk

Idealist.org
Database with over 23,000 not-for-profit and community organisations in 153 countries.
e. info@idealist.org
www.idealist.org

Indicorps
A non-partisan, non-religious organisation that encourages Indians in the UK to participate in India's progress.
t. 07973 401 522
e. info@indicorps.org
www.indicorps.org

International Service
Provides skilled people to work in organisations in Latin America, West Africa and the Middle East.
t. 01904 647 799
e. is@internationalservice.org.uk
www.internationalservice.org.uk

Merlin
Responds worldwide with vital health care for those caught up in disasters, conflict and disease.
t. 020 7065 0800
e. hq@merlin.org.uk
www.merlin.org.uk

Médècins Sans Frontières
Independent humanitarian medical aid agency.
t. 020 7404 6600
e. office-ldn@london.msf.org
www.msf.org/unitedkingdom

Raleigh International
Committed to the personal growth of young people from all nationalities and backgrounds.
t. 020 7371 8585
e. info@raleigh.org.uk
www.raleigh.org

RedR
Relieves suffering caused by disasters by providing committed personnel for humanitarian programmes.
t. 020 7233 3116
e. info@redr.org
www.redr.org/london

Skillshare
Reduces poverty and injustice and furthers economic development in partnership with communities.
t. 01162 541 862
e. info@skillshare.org
www.skillshare.org

Teach Ghana Trust
Advances education in Ghana.
e. enquiries@teachghanatrust.org.uk
www.teachghanatrust.org.uk

Trade Aid
Fights poverty by teaching vocational skills to Tanzanian people, creating sustainable employment.
t. 01425 657 774
e. info@tradeaiduk.org
www.tradeaiduk.org

United Nations Volunteers
Supports sustainable human development through volunteerism.
e. information@unvolunteers.org
www.unv.org

VSO
Voluntary work in developing countries for a wide range of professions.
t. 020 8780 7600
e. infoservices@vso.org.uk
www.vso.org.uk

Worldwide Volunteering
Provides a database of opportunities for people of any age to volunteer anywhere in the world.
t. 01935 825 588
e. wwv@wwv.org.uk
www.worldwidevolunteering.org.uk